RALF

RALF

How a Giant Schnauzer brought hope,
happiness and healing to sick children

ANNE CRAWFORD

ALLEN&UNWIN
SYDNEY·MELBOURNE·AUCKLAND·LONDON

Ralf's family are donating their share of the royalties to The Royal Children's Hospital Melbourne and Lort Smith Animal Hospital.

First published in 2015

Allen & Unwin
83 Alexander Street
Crows Nest NSW 2065
Australia
Phone: (61 2) 8425 0100
Email: info@allenandunwin.com
Web: www.allenandunwin.com

Cataloguing-in-Publication details are available
from the National Library of Australia
www.trove.nla.gov.au

ISBN 978 1 76011 122 9

Set in 13/17 pt Minion Pro by Midland Typesetters, Australia
Printed and bound in Australia by Griffin Press

10 9 8 7 6 5 4 3 2 1

CONTENTS

PROLOGUE

It was late March 2012 when Caroline Lovick discovered that the family pet, Ralf, a Giant Schnauzer, had become famous.

Ralf was a 'therapy dog' at The Royal Children's Hospital in Melbourne, padding the wards every week with Caroline, visiting young patients who were ill and injured, helping in their recovery in often remarkable ways.

A daily newspaper published a story on 20 March about the 'miracle' pooch and the effect he was having on children and adolescents, with a photo of a toddler, Zeke Harrison, who had a rare genetic disease, walking the corridors of the hospital next to the huge black dog. The article and picture of the chubby-legged infant wearing a nasal-gastric tube went from Melbourne to Sydney to newspapers in the United Kingdom and the US, and then spread on the internet. The story took off in Europe. Spain. Turkey. India. Chile. A German radio station sent a crew to Australia to record a show on Ralf. Dawn French, the British comedienne, posted Ralf on her Facebook page. A woman called Karla from Donegal sent him a gift of engraved dog tags on behalf of the people of Ireland.

Caroline had always known that there was something special about the dog that looks you directly in the eyes from beneath his shaggy forelock and bushy brows with kind brown eyes. But she wasn't prepared for this.

Ralf had gone global.

But Ralf wasn't always the animal he is today: in fact, he had once been a problem dog that attracted the attention of the local authorities in the Tasmanian town where he grew up. Ralf was a pooch that—without the extraordinary chain of events that led him to Caroline Lovick—could have had an entirely different fate.

1

A FINE
HERITAGE

Ralf or 'Erbin Gorjous Jorg', as he was named on his pedigree certificate, was born on 21 March 2004 in Ulverstone, a coastal town in northern Tasmania, in a litter of eight puppies bred by Giant Schnauzer devotee Lynda Tyzack. Ralf's mother Madison gave birth in the 'puppy room' at Lynda's home, lying in a warmed whelping box, surrounded by old carpet, newspapers, bedding, doggie dishes, toys for the pups to play with and a set of scales to monitor their growth.

Lynda was thrilled as each wriggling, healthy pup appeared; five males and three females. It was the fifth litter for Madison, a 'sweetheart' of a dog with long hair and a gentle manner, and as always, her owner hoped there would be some show prospects among them.

Before long, the pups were rollicking balls of fur with tiny razor-sharp teeth, getting up to mischief. They uprooted pot plants, tipping out the contents, tossing the plastic pots in the air and galloping around the yard with them on their noses before tearing them into tiny black pieces. They'd leap into the air to pull clothes off the line. They explored every nook and cranny in the house, looking for something to chew, an electric cord perhaps, or some paper to shred. They loved playing with the cardboard cylinders from rolls of toilet paper that Lynda would give them, chasing them around the floor then gnawing on them. They played tug-of-war with old socks that Lynda tied in knots.

There was little to distinguish the eight completely jet black pups from each other, but Lynda noticed that one had a composed air about him. A pup that was a little more relaxed than his siblings, happy to follow the mischief rather than create it. He seemed more observant too, quietly taking in whatever was happening around him. That pup, of course, would later become Ralf.

Gorjous Jorg came from a fine heritage. As close to Schnauzer royalty as you could get in Australia. Lynda had been breeding Giant Schnauzers for years; dog breeding was in her blood. She had grown up with them, going to shows with her parents when they exhibited their Dachshunds and Boxers. One of her earliest memories is of walking around a show, harnessed to the pram alongside her mother while her father managed their dogs. Her parents, John and Rayma Ritzau, were responsible for introducing some of the first Giant Schnauzers into Australia, in the 1980s. They continued to import dogs from selected bloodlines in England and the

US—the family can now lay claim to more than 300 Australian champion Schnauzers in the three sizes—Miniature, Standard and Giants—among their dogs' descendants.

Giant Schnauzers, built like tanks, and which can stand 70 centimetres at the shoulder, were originally bred in the seventeenth century as working dogs in Bavaria, Germany, where they were used to move livestock in the alps and guard farms. ('Schnauze' means snout in German.) They were acquired later by people living in towns and cities to protect stores, stockyards, breweries and factories, and were employed as military dogs in both world wars. They are now enlisted by police in European countries and as guard dogs in the US.

The cost of importing a Giant Schnauzer to Australia in the 1980s was prohibitive—thousands of dollars per dog—but John Ritzau was keen. He'd pored over photos of the 'Giants', as they're affectionately called, impressed by their grand appearance, and had heard good reports about them. The Ritzaus, who operated the Awun boarding kennels in Mornington, on the Peninsula in Victoria, already bred and showed Miniature Schnauzers. (Standard and Miniature Schnauzers had come to Australia decades before.) Their friend Audrey Ralph knew a well-established breeder in England who, along with an American woman Sylvia Hammerstrom, was fighting to save the breed; the Giants' numbers were dwindling, even in Germany. The Ritzaus bought a pregnant bitch from the Nenevale kennels, in Peterborough, eastern England, sight unseen. Nenevale had a reputation for crossing dogs from the best European bloodlines, always breeding for temperament.

'Eclipse at Nenevale' was confined to quarantine in Spotswood, Melbourne, when she arrived and her eight pups were born there. Excited as they were to learn that she'd had a litter, the Ritzaus were unable to see the pups for some weeks due to restrictions on the number of visits owners could make. 'They were busting to see them,' Lynda recalls. But four pups died in quarantine after they contracted parvovirus, a lethal disease that spreads quickly among confined animals.

The surviving pups were three months old when Lynda first saw them. She was in her early thirties at the time and had been living in northern New South Wales with her husband. The marriage was falling apart and Lynda had come to visit her parents; she would soon decide to move back home. Lynda had never met a Giant Schnauzer before. She was hooked.

The first thing that strikes people about Giant Schnauzers is their proportions. They're barrel-chested and broad-backed. Great Danes and Irish Wolfhounds are taller; Giant Schnauzers are more solid. They typically weigh anything from 34 kilograms for a female to 50 kilograms for a male. Ralf, though, tips in at 56 kilos—the weight of a small woman. Lynda says the Giants have caused near-accidents as passing motorists catch sight of her walking them around the streets of Ulverstone, while pedestrians can be seen looking at them gobsmacked or mouthing 'Oh, my god!'

But for Lynda it is the temperament of the dogs that stands out. Giant Schnauzers are good-natured and are great companions, she says. They are also very protective of their owners and their families. Lynda learned this early on during a visit to Sydney for the Royal Easter Show with her parents, staying at her grandparents' home in Beverly Hills. At the time, she was taking one of the family's dogs out for a stroll to relieve itself before bedtime. It was dark and Lynda was leading the dog,

Fluffy, who was from the first litter, around the streets when three drunk men veered across the road and headed towards her. Fluffy slowly and deliberately put his body in front of Lynda's, planted all four legs, and gave a long, guttural growl. The men quickly 'sobered up' at the sight of the black hulk and hastily made their way back over to the other side of the road.

When Lynda takes her dogs to Melbourne on the *Spirit of Tasmania*, she is always amused as she watches the burly security guards shrinking at the sight of her pets and steering a wide berth around them. The dogs look and sound ferocious but it's all bravado, she says. Madison, for instance, once saw a pint-sized pug coming towards her at a dog show as she sat next to Lynda waiting to compete—and crawled under Lynda's fold-up chair to escape it.

Lynda discovered another trait shared by the breed: they have an independent streak. 'You can see them thinking,' she says. 'You'll tell them not to do something and they'll think of another equally naughty way of doing it. They're also intelligent—if you don't train a Schnauzer, it will train you.'

She was given her first Giant Schnauzer, a bitch called Grace, by her parents as a present to kick-start her own dog breeding and showing career. Grace, Ralf's great-great-great-grandmother, was a 'charming old girl' who'd proved herself in the show ring as an Australian Champion and was past showing. She would have one last litter before she was retired from breeding, too. Lynda started showing the pups from that litter when they were seven or eight months old. Later she bred from the females she kept from each litter, carefully and conscientiously, spacing the litters out to give the mothers a long rest in between. She bred for temperament; show-quality was good, temperament was essential. Lynda, a no-nonsense woman with a quiet sense of humour, breeds dogs because she enjoys the process, playing with the pups and finding homes for them, and shows them only to enhance their reputation. 'I love it when my dogs win but I'm not a very serious competitor—it's not winning cattle stations.'

She screens the people who want to buy her pups—as far as is possible—to make sure they can provide the right home; that they have a safe, secure backyard, will exercise the dog regularly, spend time with it, and have company for it. Training is important, she stresses—Giant Schnauzers can dominate if they're not disciplined early. Socialising a pup with people and other animals from a young age is vital, too.

'But once a dog is sold, it's out of your hands; you can't control what people do with their dogs,' she says.

Lynda has sold Schnauzer pups to people all over Australia and in New Zealand. A Perth man who'd been blind since he was seven years old, yet was mobile, wanted one as a pet. His wife was blind, too, and suffered short-term memory loss. That dog saved them both from danger and distress many times over. When the wife collapsed near the toilet one night while her husband was sleeping, the dog went into the couple's room, woke the man up, took his wrist in her mouth and led him to where the woman lay. She would stand behind the husband at the automatic teller machine of his local bank and warn off anyone thinking of taking advantage of an obviously blind man. And she caught Perth's number-one burglar when she was only nine months old . . .

It was the late 1990s and the notorious house-breaker had scaled the couple's tall metal fence one night and was no doubt sizing up the back windows and doors when the young dog cornered him in the garage. The husband rang the police to tell them that his dog had an intruder bailed up although he hadn't seen them.

'How do you know there's someone in there?' asked the policeman.

'Because I can tell from the sounds that the garage door is up and it was locked earlier,' the man replied. 'And the dog won't come in when I call her—she's guarding us.'

The police, who'd been trying to catch the criminal for some time, were even more impressed when they found out after they'd arrested the man that he'd been caught by a nine-month-old pup, something they made known later at the jail where the man was incarcerated—without mentioning how big the pup had been. They admitted quietly, though, that they'd been scared of her themselves.

Many Schnauzers, large and small, have passed through Lynda's hands over the years. Hers is a doggie household. Dogs come first, she says, everyone knows that. There are rarely less than four in the house at any one time, always the sound of a dog snoring or snuffling, the rapid rat-a-tat-tat of paws on wood, enthusiastic panting or the occasional bark. Huge sashes won at shows with shiny gold titles are draped over furniture. Trophies sit on the top of a fireplace, plaques and ribbons lie scattered among the clutter of her living room. A framed head-and-shoulders portrait of a Schnauzer sits waiting to be hung; silhouettes of Schnauzers adorn the fridge.

RALF

Lynda sells the pups she breeds always with the proviso that she'll take a dog back and rehome it if it doesn't work out. But of all the dogs that have passed through her hands over the years, she has had only one that proved a problem. And that dog was Ralf's father.

2

RALF'S FATHER

Ralf's father Davey was a handsome young dog, a tall, solid boy with an outgoing nature. Lynda sold him to a family she thought would make fine owners—the husband was familiar with Giant Schnauzers and was keen to own one, although his wife and children had favoured getting a smaller dog. Soon after they bought their new pet, however, the husband's work circumstances changed and he was away at his job for long periods of time, leaving the family with the dog. Within four months they had a pup almost the height of a full-grown dog on their hands. The wife and children couldn't cope with his size, became frightened of him and left him alone in the backyard. She would open the back door and throw food out to him when he needed feeding. Davey became nervous and fearful.

A few months later, Lynda heard that the wife wasn't able to control the dog and offered to take him back and find another home for him.

When Lynda arrived and was taken through to the backyard, she found a quivering, anxious animal that didn't recognise her and had to be pushed and pulled out to her car. 'There was no aggression, he was just absolutely terrified.'

Once back at Ulverstone, Davey relaxed, remembering his former owner and the other dogs. For a while Lynda thought of keeping him. 'You're not such a bad boy,' she told him, looking at his eager face. But an older bitch that was protective of Lynda took a disliking to him, trying to attack him whenever he got too close, and Lynda knew she'd have to move him on. She didn't know of anybody who wanted a grown Giant Schnauzer at the time, only small puppies, so was pleased to hear from a woman who was interested, perhaps having heard through kennel club circles that there was a Giant Schnauzer going. The woman was a well-known breeder who wanted a sire. She asked Lynda why she was trying to rehome the dog and listened as she explained how he'd become a problem. The woman said all the right things in reply. She sounded perfect.

But she rang Lynda after a month to say that Davey had bitten her and she was sending him back. 'He's going to bite someone else,' she warned.

Lynda didn't know what she was going to find when she arrived to pick the dog up, yet he greeted her like a long-lost friend, jumping up and licking her, a 'G'day, Mum, I'm back' greeting, as Lynda puts it. But when she got Davey home, Lynda found that his behaviour had deteriorated even more. He would be affectionate one minute then snap at her without reason the next when he was around other people and dogs. Ralf's father stayed with Lynda for ten days before she had him put down. It was a horrible decision to have to make, she says. But you can't take a chance with a big dog like that. You can't have a Giant Schnauzer on the front page of a tabloid newspaper for all the wrong reasons.

Davey was just a lovely dog whose life had gone bad after the wrong treatment, she says. But Lynda knew the bloodlines were sound and took the step of having the dog's semen frozen before he died, later to be implanted in 'Causin' a Storm', or Madison. And that was where Ralf had his beginning.

3

PUPPYHOOD

Madison's pups thrived in their first weeks of life, gaining weight and becoming bolder by the day. They had been weaned off their mother and were ready for their new lives elsewhere when Lynda's world took a tumble. One night in May 2004 when the pups were seven weeks old, Lynda misjudged a back step at her home in Tasmania, fell and landed heavily on the ground. She knew as soon as she heard the sharp crack that she'd broken her leg. Lynda was taken by a friend to the Mersey Community Hospital, thinking on the way that she'd be treated that night and be home in plaster the next day. But instead she learned that it was a bad break, a major 'spiral crack' running down the tibia bone of her lower leg, and that X-rays revealed she'd chipped a bone in her ankle, too—she'd be in hospital for at least a week and off her feet for months.

With her leg in plaster from hip to toe, Lynda would not be able to walk, bend down to feed the dogs or pick up the pups. She had nine dogs to look after; two Miniature Schnauzers, Madison and six active puppies that needed care. Two pups had already been sold. Lynda knew she had to find homes for the others quickly, but worried about what to do with them in the meantime. She was unable to afford to pay to board all the dogs in kennels, which usually refused to take puppies anyway because they were more prone to infection. Her partner at the time, Peter, had dogs of his own and couldn't take on any more.

Dog breeders are a close-knit bunch, especially in a small show circuit like Tasmania, and fortunately a friend and fellow dog-lover stepped in to help.

Lynda had met Jenny Moore on the state's show circuit a few years earlier. Both women had started showing at about the same time and both had recently moved to northern Tasmania—Lynda from Victoria, and Jenny returning to the state after living in Brisbane for twenty-five years. Jenny, who lived about an hour away to the east, bred Schipperkes, small black dogs with pointy ears and a ruffle of fur around their necks. Schipperkes originally came from Belgium where they often lived on canal boats, hence the name that translates as 'little skipper'. Jenny was intrigued by the appearance of the Giant Schnauzers at the shows she competed in, and she and

Lynda got talking. The breed was rare in Tasmania—Lynda knew of only a few dogs kept as pets elsewhere in the state.

Not long before Lynda broke her leg, Jenny had arranged to visit her to look at her latest litter. Jenny was taken by what she saw: shaggy bundles of long soft fur and big floppy ears, playing and falling over their own feet. She talked to Lynda about taking one on as a show dog. In the dog-showing world, taking on someone else's show dog as an exhibitor is not uncommon: the dog stays in the owner's name and the exhibitor looks after it, paying for all its expenses. Breeders want their dogs shown to maintain a profile and to improve the breeding credentials of their animals, even if they don't own them anymore. Terms are worked out beforehand— usually the deal is that the owner is given the first litter from the bitch and the exhibitor then keeps the bitch. Lynda was keen on the idea, too: it meant she could keep one dog from the litter to be shown without having to look after it, and she liked Jenny.

Jenny, for her part, thought it would be good to show another breed, as well as the Schipperkes. There were often long periods of time spent waiting between classes at shows or between winning a section and the final judging of an overall category. She liked, too, the idea of learning about a breed that was so different to that of her own dogs. Schipperkes are the size of Miniature Schnauzers, weighing only 3 to 9 kilograms and have a livelier, more independent nature.

The women had arranged for Jenny to visit Lynda's house on a Saturday to select a pup. Ralf was not a likely candidate, though—there were better show prospects among the litter. Ralf's ears stuck out whereas they should have dropped flat from the temples in triangles—he was destined to be a pet, Lynda thought.

The night before Jenny was due to visit, she was surprised to pick up the phone and hear Lynda's voice. 'Better not worry about coming around tomorrow,' Lynda said. 'I'm in the Mersey hospital—I've broken my leg!' she added, almost flippantly.

Jenny phoned Lynda back at the hospital the next day to find out how her friend was faring. Lynda had more bad news: the break had turned out to be worse than the doctors initially thought and she now faced months of being in plaster. She seemed rather matter-of-fact about the ordeal until Jenny asked about the dogs, when a worried tone took over. There was no one at home to care for the dogs, Lynda explained. The Miniature Schnauzers could go to some kennels run by friends in Devonport and Madison could stay with a friend, but as for the puppies?

Jenny did go over to her friend's house that afternoon—but instead of taking one puppy home, she took six.

Peter was there when she arrived and showed her through to the puppy room. It was only twenty-four hours since Lynda had gone to hospital but the pens were already a mess and the puppies, who hadn't been out, were manic. Jenny and Peter carried them out, two by two, to Jenny's car. As she drove home, Jenny wondered just what she'd got herself in for.

She already had five Schipperkes to look after but was equipped to handle a few more dogs—at least until Lynda sold them. Her one-hectare property had seven kennels with seven runs, a big backyard and an old stable that had been Schipperke-proofed. Jenny rearranged her dogs so that three Giant Schnauzer pups could go into each of the two larger enclosures.

The daughter of dairy farmers on King Island growing up with livestock and dogs, Jenny says she needs to be surrounded by animals. At one stage in Brisbane she owned nine Schipperkes. She'd acquired and bred the dogs after falling in love with a pup in the window of a pet shop in early 1999—at the age of forty-four. Jenny, a sensible, contained woman by her own reckoning, admits it was an impulse buy. 'I bought him for all the wrong reasons!' she says, with a laugh. 'Ace' came with a pedigree and papers; Jenny had no intention of exhibiting him but met some people who encouraged her to show. She returned to King Island from Brisbane in early 2001 to care for her mother, who had cancer, in the last few months of her life. Jenny's father, sadly, had died the year before.

On the first weekend that she had the Schnauzer pups, she took them up to her house so that she could handle each one individually. She bought each pup a different-coloured collar to distinguish it and gave them temporary names: Miss Green, Mr Blue, Mr Zebra Print, and so on. She bathed them with the help of a friend who was a dog show judge and had offered to assess them as potential show dogs. Her friend looked at each pup, felt them all over and commented on their proportions and coats: 'This one's a bit long in the body', 'This one's too tall for his age', and so on. The two women spent the afternoon caring for the litter and, as they did, one of the pups stood out for Jenny; a relaxed male, 'a real softy'. There was something funny about his mannerisms; just looking at him made you smile, she recalls. 'He would look you in the eyes and you knew there was an intelligent being in there,' Jenny says. She fell for the good-natured pup in the red collar. She would later name him Ralf.

In the weeks that followed, Jenny watched the six pups as they developed; playing, rolling and tumbling with each other, pretend-fighting, bounding around clumsily, chewing whatever they could find, pouncing with their front legs then springing up again and racing around, chasing birds flying impossibly high above them, then flopping down to sleep, and sleep some more. They were developing muscles and working out a pecking order among their pack—the relaxed Ralf was definitely not at the top! They careered around Jenny's tidy backyard, dug holes and left bare patches in the lawn. It was a cold, wet Tasmanian winter and Jenny was constantly drying the pups and wiping mud off them. But she didn't mind any of it—it was a delight to have them there.

When the pups were three months old, Jenny took them to the vet for their second vaccinations, running in and out of the surgery from her car carrying one lumpen pup at a time. Lynda, meanwhile, had found good homes for them; before long the pups would be leaving. Jenny then made several trips to the freight office of the Launceston airport where the young dogs were put onto planes bound for Victoria, Western Australia or Queensland. She always felt a pang of anxiety as they were wheeled off in their crates, along with the luggage, to be put in the cargo hold, wondering what it was like in there and knowing they'd be frightened of the strange environment. But at least she had her dog.

To her credit, Lynda, instead of picking the best pup for Jenny to show on her behalf, let her choose the one she wanted. After all, Jenny had been kind enough to look after the pups for Lynda, and it was clear that her friend had bonded with the pup in the red collar.

Several months later Ralf was approaching his full height, so tall that the Schipperkes could walk underneath him. He treated them carefully, lying on the ground with his paws out in front of him as they played around him. Visitors more used to seeing Schipperkes at Jenny's house were amused at the sight of the new addition. When Jenny had friends to lunch, Ralf would sit on the step outside the rear sliding door, looking hopefully in the window, shiny eyed, mouth open, grinning. Jenny had never thought too much about Ralf's 'cheesy grin' until a friend commented on it one day.

But the man who came to buy a water tank that Jenny had advertised in the local paper saw another side to Ralf.

Jenny greeted the man at her front door when he arrived and motioned to the rear yard, warning him to 'Just wait here while I'll put the Schnauzer away'. But he ignored her and walked towards the picket gate to the backyard. As he did, Ralf rushed towards the gate, leapt up at it and issued a few deep barks. The man jumped back a metre. Ralf, standing with his big heavy paws hanging on the top of the gate, looked equally surprised, as if to say, 'Well, what do I do now?'

'I told you to wait,' Jenny said to the embarrassed man, privately amused and rather proud of her would-be guard dog.

4

RALF HITS THE SHOW RING

Jenny started showing Ralf when he was six months old. As soon as she did, people who knew her started quipping, 'Good grief! What are you feeding that Schipperke?' or 'What sort of shampoo are you using on that dog?' Ralf was large but immature; an oversized pup that hadn't grown into himself. He had reached his full height but had yet to bulk out and develop what Jenny calls the 'oomph factor' that adult male Giant Schnauzers have.

Ralf's first show was at the Brighton Kennel Club, north of Hobart, in September 2004. He was quite content to go along with it all, waiting with Jenny near the ring to compete in their first event, enjoying the attention of being patted by people who came over to say hello. Jenny, however, was less relaxed—showing a Giant Schnauzer was new territory for her; she didn't know the breed and wasn't sure how Ralf would rate, although she had pored over the guidelines set by the governing body, the Australian National Kennel Club.

The ANKC sets 'breed standards' for Schnauzers—guidelines that describe the ideal characteristics, temperament, and appearance of a dog (or bitch) and ensure that it is sound, following those set by the Kennel Club in England. They specify that Giant Schnauzers, classed as 'utility dogs', should be powerfully built, robust, sinewy, appearing almost square, imposing, with a keen expression and alert attitude. In terms of characteristics, they should be versatile, strong, hardy, intelligent, vigorous, adaptable, capable of great speed and endurance and 'resistant to weather'.

Correct conformation is of the utmost importance—and this is where Jenny worried about Ralf. The head should be strong, moderately broad between the ears with a flat creaseless forehead, have a powerful muzzle ending in a blunt wedge, with bristly stubby moustache and chin whiskers, and bushy eyebrows. So far, so good. However, a Giant Schnauzer's ears should be neat, V-shaped, set high and drop forward to the temple. This, Lynda had flagged, would be Ralf's downfall. As a young dog, his ears stuck out.

Teeth must conform to 'a perfect, regular and complete scissor bite'. Desirable lips are black and close tightly without overlapping. More ticks for Ralf.

The ideal Giant Schnauzer has a neck that is moderately long, strong and slightly arched, shoulders are flat and well laid back, and forelegs straight. The chest should be broad and deep with a conspicuous forechest. It has a strong, straight back, which should be well muscled. Giant Schnauzers have coats that are pure black or 'pepper and salt' in colour—white markings on the head, chest and legs are a no-no. The animal's topcoat should be harsh and wiry. A dark facial mask is essential.

The breed standards also describe how the dogs should move—with a gait that's free, balanced and vigorous. Their height is decreed: variations outside 65–70 centimetres for dogs and 60–65 centimetres for bitches are undesirable. And the male's testicles get a mention (must have two, fully descended into the scrotum).

And that's just the abridged list.

The guidelines note that any departure from the ANKC standards should be considered a 'fault' and the 'seriousness with which the fault is regarded should be in exact proportion to its degree and its effect on the health and welfare of the dog'.

Says Jenny, 'I just knew that I had a healthy dog.'

She had discovered that the amount of grooming needed to show a Giant Schnauzer was far more than she'd thought.

Schnauzers must be 'stripped' on the upper body some weeks before a show, a time-consuming process in which the hair is plucked out then allowed to grow back again so the coat is as flat and tight as possible. A metal comb is held against four fingers while the thumb is pressed against the hair, which is then ripped out by the roots with a flick of the wrist. This helps shape the coat to the desired look.

'It doesn't leave holes in the dog!' Jenny jokes, adding that Ralf didn't seem to mind being stripped.

Each part of the body then has to be trimmed to perfection immediately before the show; the 'trousers' tidied, the facial hair shaped to accentuate the Schnauzer's distinguished eyebrows and whiskers and so that it has the desired 'brick-shaped head', as Lynda puts it. The hairs on the dog's legs must be trimmed to make the legs look as cylindrical as possible, 'like a barber's pole'. The nails are clipped, ears tidied, tummy hair snipped to run at a nice angle from the chest down, and the hairs on the dog's back made level. Some exhibitors use hairspray for the final touches and whip out a comb in the ring to fluff up a furnishing—the hair hanging off the belly and from the legs—or flatten some stray hairs.

Owners have to make sure they're well groomed, too, wearing pants that highlight the dark shades of their dogs and maybe a smart jacket.

Dogs are judged on conformation, coat and bearing rather than behaviour; however, if a dog is badly behaved—say, jumping up on a judge or growling at them when having its gums examined—it and its owner will be 'excused' from the ring.

Jenny grew more nervous the longer she waited, looking at Ralf all over and wondering if she'd prepared him properly and would handle him in the correct way. She had showing Schipperkes down to a tee, but there were different rules for Schnauzers—for example, an exhibitor is allowed to hold up a Schnauzer's head and arrange its legs so that the dog is standing squarely and the judge can see that it has a straight back. She hoped that Ralf wouldn't do anything untoward. Puppies have been known to roll over in front of a judge, jump up and grab parts of their clothing such as a dangling scarf or tie, refuse to walk once they're in the ring, gallop around when they're meant to be walking, and cock a leg or squat in front of a judge even though they've just been taken for a pee by the owner beforehand. And then there was Ralf's overall presentation—had she fluffed up the right bits of his coat?

Eventually she and Ralf were called into the ring, which was actually rectangular like many of the show rings. Jenny watched anxiously as the judge measured Ralf's face to see that the length of his snout was in proportion to its width, opened his mouth to check his teeth, and checked under his furnishings for straight bones. The judge then viewed the pup from all angles, bending down for a better look, and inspected his scrotum. Ralf behaved well, though he wanted to sit down and relax instead of standing, as is required, and tried to look around to see what else was going on rather than giving his handler and the judge his undivided attention.

Finalists in all events are asked to run their dog so that the judge can observe the dog's gait. Ralf obliged.

At the end of the judging, Ralf won Best of Breed. It was, in fact, a predicted result: Ralf had no competition—there were no other Giant Schnauzers in his class.

A few weeks later, Ralf stood out for all the wrong reasons at the Ulverstone Agricultural Show.

It was a balmy September day and he was waiting in one of Jenny's show trolleys on the football oval where the annual event was held. Jenny had wheeled the trolley—a hip-height, metal-framed box on four wheels—halfway across the field towards sheds at one end that were used by competitors, when she decided to visit the toilet, leaving Ralf in the trolley. He was sitting contentedly, she thought, though he took up most of the trolley. She turned and walked towards the toilet block.

But Ralf took umbrage at being left, pushed up the lid and jumped out. Jenny was barely gone a few minutes but as she was walking back she heard a commotion and cries of '*Loose dog! Loose dog!*' She was startled to see her empty trolley and no Ralf.

Jenny knew he wouldn't run amok but there was always the chance that any unrestrained dog might approach other dogs and get in a fight, or walk in front of a car. Moreover, it was considered extremely bad etiquette to let your dog loose. Errant owners can be banned from exhibiting for six months for doing this, she says. Jenny had once seen two handlers whose dogs—a St Bernard and a bulldog—took exception to each other from across adjoining rings, on the ground almost on their bellies trying to stop their animals from reaching each other. She remembers too, the horrified faces of the spectators as Daisy the Schipperke escaped and trotted into the ring on the heels of another dog Jenny was showing.

Jenny soon spotted Ralf strolling the perimeter of the oval, casually looking around. *Where's she gone? Who'll pat me next? Perhaps there'll be some food over there?* Jenny approached and called out; Ralf meandered over to her, happy to see her but oblivious to his misdemeanour. *What do you mean escape? I was just having a talk to everybody.*

Jenny used a strap to secure her trolleys from then on.

She showed Ralf in eight shows over the next three months, entering him in Puppy Class, and also exhibiting the

Schipperkes in their categories. Ralf never disgraced himself, though Jenny wondered whether his lack of animation in the ring counted against him—a show dog was meant to look spirited. As other owners tried to contain their dog's excitement before they were shown, Ralf would doze off. Jenny would have to wake, and enliven him.

Once, Ralf fell asleep on the grooming table when the judging started earlier than planned. 'Wake up, Ralf! Come on, let's go!' Jenny urged, as Ralf took his time to get to his feet and move. He moseyed into the ring and despite Jenny's best efforts to rouse him, still looked indifferent. 'If you're a good show dog, you're meant to look like you enjoy it!' she told him.

With virtually no competition, Ralf would win the Best in Breed section but never the Best in Group where he'd have to compete against other dogs in the 'utility' class; Schnauzers of various sizes, Dobermans, Boxers, Samoyeds, Siberian Huskies and St Bernards among them. And the prospect of Ralf ever becoming Best in Show wasn't even a remote possibility. Best in Show is the ultimate contest in which the winning dogs from each category (hounds, terriers, utility dogs, etc.) compete against each other, judged on which dog best represents its type.

Sometimes Jenny blamed her own handling or grooming but deep down she knew the real cause: Ralf just wasn't the best choice of show dog. He was an amenable, middle-of-the-road competitor, she says. 'He was never going to be Best in Show or a glamour dog. They were just humouring me, letting me show him!'

Jenny, however, is not a fiercely competitive person so it

didn't worry her too much. 'Any Schipperke who fails as a show dog I keep and love,' she says.

Some breeders maintain that if a dog's not going to win in the show ring, that it should not be bred from, and that puppies with conformation faults should be put down. Serious competitors on the Australian circuit take their dogs to a show almost every weekend. Some employ professional handlers and dog groomers for the events, and bring their own tents to house the dogs while they're being prepared, complete with grooming tables and generators to run hairdryers.

Jenny later saw how the even more ambitious exhibitors did it when she and Lynda went to the famous Crufts dog fair in Birmingham, England, in 2007. Crufts attracts 22,000 dogs and their owners over its four days, all of them vying for the Best in Show prize, the dog enthusiasts' holy grail. The best Giant Schnauzer in the show—'a magnificent, big strong dog that looked sharp and smart and had the right attitude in the show ring,' according to Jenny—was managed seven days a week by a married couple. The husband oversaw the dog's exercise at home, running with it for several hours each day so that its muscles were perfectly defined; the wife did the daily grooming.

'As someone who works full-time I wouldn't have a hope of emulating that kind of care,' Jenny says. 'That's what made that dog world famous.'

Despite his lack of show prowess, Ralf continued to entertain Jenny at home. She would look on charmed by some new antic and marvel at his unfolding intelligence.

But Jenny learned early that Ralf couldn't be trusted around food. He would sit by the dining table, his head at table height, and help himself to food from her plate as soon she went out of the room. She gave up trying to train him not to hang around the table at mealtimes and put him outside whenever she had visitors. One day when Ralf had been inside with her, Jenny realised that the house had gone suspiciously quiet. She looked around the kitchen and living room then outside its large window to see Ralf in a far corner of the backyard, looking down intently. She walked into the backyard in time to see him with his muzzle in a container of gourmet butter. The container had been sitting beside the cooktop; Jenny had left the kitchen and Ralf had snatched it, taking the whole thing outside to devour its contents. When Jenny went to retrieve the container, by now licked clean, Ralf stood looking up at her with whiskers coated in butter. 'He was so pleased with himself!'

Most of all, Ralf loved people. Jenny's Schipperkes were fairly independent dogs, happy in their own company; Ralf wanted to be with people all the time. He sought out visitors, amusing them with his cheesy grin and amiable, gentlemanly manner. He always wanted to be inside; being put outside was like a punishment to him. When Jenny had guests over for a meal, Ralf was put outside and would bark loudly, upset at being ignored. And being left alone was worse.

5

TROUBLE

Jenny left Ralf in the backyard with one of the Schipperkes for company when she went to work as a librarian during the day, putting the other Schipperkes in their kennels. She let the dogs inside before work to spend time with her and at night when she got home. Ralf always looked mournful when she took him outside before departing each morning, putting on his best sad face, but as far as Jenny knew he coped with being left.

Then in late December 2004—about seven months after she'd taken Ralf on—Jenny answered a knock on the door and was confronted by a woman wearing a shirt that identified her as being from Northern Midlands Council. The council officer told Jenny that her nearest neighbour had lodged a complaint against 'the Airedale', mistaking Ralf for another big breed, and asked Jenny if she could make an appointment to come back and 'see about things'.

'Come in now,' said Jenny.

'I need to make an appointment,' insisted the council officer. It sounded ominously official.

They made an appointment for the following Monday morning, 31 December.

Jenny was taken aback but not completely surprised at the news—she knew the neighbours didn't like her dogs.

The house in Perth had come as a dream home for Jenny as a breeder—on a large block overhung with graceful gums and old fruit trees, with plenty of room for the dogs to exercise and seven existing kennels with runs to boot. She made it a condition of purchase that the property came with a licence to own seven dogs. The only drawback seemed to be the trucking company to one side of the property, out of which logging trucks would rumble in the very early morning.

But her joy in finding the house was short-lived. Jenny didn't see eye-to-eye with the neighbours on the other side from the time she moved in. She was off to a bad start when Peppi, her mother's poodle, which she looked after for a while, escaped, ran into the neighbours' backyard and chased the woman living there. There was much activity and noise next door at times, which set the Schipperkes off barking, which in turn provoked the neighbours into shouting at the dogs from the other side of the fence. 'I kind of felt that my small dogs' noises were less than the truck noises,' Jenny says. The neighbours—who have since moved and been replaced by 'lovely' people who don't mind Jenny's pets—felt otherwise. And when Ralf started barking in his resounding voice, it was the last straw. One day when she was speaking on the phone to Lynda, and Ralf barked, the man from next door screamed out menacingly at her from over the fence, 'The big dog has to go!'

Jenny was unaware that Ralf barked while she was at work—he didn't make a sound as she went out to her car each morning. But there was another issue: Jenny was licensed to have seven 'compact' dogs on the property. She had five Schipperkes and hoped that she'd get away with keeping a larger dog too. 'I was in deep trouble—I had a permit for the other dogs but not for Ralf. It was my fault.'

The council officer returned as agreed to talk about the situation.

'I offered to show her around the place and she saw how well kept the dogs are.' But it was the number and type of dogs that was the concern, not how they were kept.

The council told her she had until the end of January to get Ralf off the property. The Tasmanian Dog Act 2000 specifies under Section 46 that a court can rule that dogs creating a nuisance, including dogs that persistently bark, can be destroyed or removed from the premises of those in charge of them.

Jenny was stricken. She'd cared for Ralf as best she could and thought that having another dog with him when she was away would provide enough company to stop him getting anxious or bored. Now she realised that he wasn't getting the attention he needed. Ralf needed to be in a home with people around all day. She made the agonising decision to let him go.

Jenny Moore isn't a person who cries easily but she sobbed as she talked to Lynda on the phone about giving Ralf back.

Lynda promised her friend that she would find him a good home—somewhere he would be surrounded by people all day. She reassured Jenny that she often had people calling to see if she had any dogs for sale.

'He was still in Lynda's name and she took it on as her problem,' Jenny says.

But Lynda worried privately about Ralf.

He'd been well looked after by Jenny and was sound in nature—but people contacting her about buying a dog invariably wanted a puppy. They were wary of older dogs that were being given away, asking themselves, 'What's wrong with it? What sort of problems am I going to inherit?'

She contacted a couple of people who she knew wanted a Giant Schnauzer but they told her they didn't want an adult dog. She thought of a Melbourne family, the Lovicks, who had approached her a while back but recalled that they'd asked for a puppy, too, so discounted them.

The council's deadline of the end of January was fast approaching. Jenny was nevertheless surprised to hear from Lynda one day that she'd organised a new home for Ralf with a family in Melbourne. The family, the Lovicks, had previously owned one of Lynda's dogs and knew about Giant Schnauzers. Lynda had called them on the off chance that they'd take on an older male pup—rather than a young female—and they'd agreed.

Jenny was relieved to learn that Ralf would be going to a good home. But she still cried on the evening of Friday 27 January after she met Lynda at the Devonport ferry terminal, where Lynda would board a boat bound for Melbourne. She said her goodbyes to Ralf and handed him over.

Trouble

The following day, Jenny was pleased to hear Lynda's account of Ralf's arrival at his new home. Lynda had stayed for a while to settle him in, but Ralf seemed content to be there. He didn't take so much as a second glance when she left. Jenny was delighted that Ralf had gone to a home he deserved. 'He was just a lovely dog, a gentle, big bloke,' she says.

She missed him for a long time afterwards.

6

THE FAMILY

Sam and Caroline Lovick had been married for fifteen years and had four children by the time they decided to buy their first dog in 2000. The couple, who'd both grown up near Warwick, the county town of Warwickshire in England's Midlands, had moved several times between the UK, the US and Australia— there'd never been a time before then when they were settled enough to add a canine member to the family.

Sam had been raised in a family that was never without a dog, whether it was a mutt given to his father (a doctor), by a patient in lieu of paying a medical bill or as a gift, or a rescue animal his twin brother Joe had brought home. Sam's good-hearted mother also contributed, adopting a German Shepherd from the Animal Protection League that they called Twig because she was so thin when they got her.

Caroline, on the other hand, never had a dog as a child, although the family owned a one-eyed cat called Prudence. For her, it was always horses—she was a competitive rider. Dogs became part of her life when she became Sam's high-school sweetheart at sixteen. She remembers particularly his family's Boxer, Diggery, who'd run off in the woods when Sam and Joe were taking him for a walk, leaving them to search for him. Diggery took a liking to Caroline, and would sit on her lap while she was watching television, but whenever she tried to stand up to go home, the dog would make a low grumbling sound and Sam would have to get up and call him so Caroline could leave.

The couple married and lived in London, both working for Neil Kinnock's Labour Party for a while before Sam, who'd studied medicine yet was keen on computers, found his niche doing economic modelling for a new economics firm in London. He often travelled overseas for his job, was promoted, and in the early nineties was asked to open a new branch in Melbourne. In 1993, Sam and Caroline moved to Australia with Alice, aged five, and Imogen, two. They settled into a house in Kew, a well-established suburb of inner Melbourne. Rebecca was born in 1995 and Edward in 1996. When Edward was still a baby, the family shifted to Concord, Massachusetts, for Sam's work, but returned to Australia the following year.

So it was back to Kew where they rented a large cream brick house not far from their previous home. It was while they were living in this house that they thought a family dog might be in order. But there was another reason why they wanted a dog— and a big dog. The Lovicks were burgled three times within three months in Kew. On the first occasion the thieves broke into the house while the family slept and took a handbag and Sam's computer. The second robbery was even more worrying: nine-year-old Alice noticed the following morning that her school laptop was no longer on the dining room table. When Caroline suggested it might be in her bedroom, Alice pointed to a boot print on the yellow couch near the window. A few minutes later, they discovered that the intruders had also stolen items from the children's bedside tables while they slept. Caroline didn't sleep well after that.

The third time, Caroline suspected she heard something outside, pulled back a curtain to check and was confronted by a man standing there. She shouted to Sam and the man ran off. When the couple reported the attempted burglary to the police the next day, they were told that the house wasn't secure and that alarms wouldn't help.

'Go out and get a big black dog,' the police officer said.

'I'll get twelve big black dogs if that's what I need,' said Caroline.

And so it was settled. The Lovicks would get a new companion for the children as well as a deterrent to would-be thieves. Caroline didn't have a preference for a breed, though Sam wanted a Bull Mastiff (the big, tan chunky dogs with drooping jowls) and the children a Bernese Mountain Dog (large, fluffy and tricoloured) because they fancied these dogs and knew people who owned them.

A chance encounter helped them narrow the choice.

Caroline was shopping in Kew one day with Rebecca, who was three, and Edward, two, and was coming out of the supermarket when she noticed a huge black dog tied up outside.

The family

As she made her way out of the store, Rebecca and Ed took off and ran towards the dog, by now excited and straining on its lead towards the children. Caroline couldn't move fast enough to stop them, as they hurled themselves on the dog, hugging it. She panicked. Then looked on incredulously as the dog allowed the children to cuddle it while it sat there, quietly, next to its owner. The woman, who Caroline guessed was a little older than herself, smiled at her pet adoringly. 'Isn't he just gorgeous?' she said to the children.

Caroline caught her breath and apologised to the woman.

'I have no idea why they did it,' she said. 'They know they're not allowed to pat dogs without asking their owners first.'

The woman assured Caroline that she knew her dog well and that he would never harm a child. Caroline looked down at the trio on the ground; the dog seemed to be soaking up the children's affection. She started talking to the woman about her dog and learned that he was a Giant Schnauzer. She asked about the breed, explaining her family's recent decision to get a large dog.

'If ever there's a dog you need, it's one of these,' the woman said. They talked about the temperament of the breed and the considerations of owning a dog that size. And they don't 'shed', the woman said, stroking the dog's coarse coat. Caroline became even more interested.

She was unaware that there were dogs that *didn't* drop hair (or very little hair). The woman explained that some breeds, like Schnauzers, had such coats. This not only saves their owners from having to wear clothes constantly flecked with dog hair but is good for people with allergies—an important consideration as Alice had an allergy that could be set off by fur.

Caroline eventually prised her reluctant children off the dog and thanked the woman, who had passed on the name of the dog's breeder, Lynda Tyzack. She went home and after talking to Sam, phoned the breeder that evening.

At the time Lynda was living in a cottage in The Gurdies, a small, hilly bush settlement south of Melbourne. She'd moved there after her parents sold the boarding kennels in Mornington. The two-bedroom cottage, made of the type of grey concrete blocks used to build dairy farms, was sold as a deceased estate. It needed work but it suited Lynda. She renovated and added decking that made the most of the views of Western Port Bay below, and fenced off a large backyard for her dogs.

Lynda's breeding female, Grace, was expecting a litter of puppies in three weeks when Caroline Lovick called her. Caroline told Lynda that the family was in the process of looking for a dog, and that she'd met one of Lynda's Giant Schnauzers at the local supermarket. She explained that they specifically needed a dog that didn't set off her daughter's allergies. Could they come down and meet the expectant mother for ten minutes to test Alice out with her? Lynda thought the request was unusual but she sensed that Caroline was genuinely interested and agreed.

The following Saturday after swimming lessons, the Lovicks piled into the car for the trip to Lynda's, the children chattering excitedly the whole way. They'd owned hermit crabs, goldfish, a hamster and a pet rat before, but because they'd moved so often, hadn't been able to care for a cat or dog. When they arrived, Caroline was immediately struck by how dog-oriented Lynda's household was—dusty paw prints everywhere, the dogs were relaxing contentedly in the sunroom, layers of newspaper covering parts of the floor. Lynda's love of her dogs reminded her of Sam's mother. Caroline warmed to her immediately.

The children, however, could focus on only one thing: the pregnant Giant Schnauzer. Grace was shaggy, rotund with a dangling belly and protruding teats. They thought she was just beautiful.

But Lynda let the Lovicks know that she wasn't going to sell one of her pups to just *any* family. Giant Schnauzers needed special care, she said. For a start, there would have to be someone at home all the time to look after the pup when it was small so that it had company. They were greedy, they'd eat anything, so you had to be careful not to overfeed them, especially when they were young. And you shouldn't over-exercise them when they were still growing because too much exertion would put a strain on their hips. Lynda discussed in detail with Sam and Caroline what would be involved in caring for the dog, then had a firm word to the four children.

'Looking after this puppy is really important,' she told them. 'You've got to do whatever Mum says. You can't leave your toys on the floor or the puppy will chew them. And everyone has to clean up after the pup.'

Alice, Rebecca, Imogen and Ed looked at her wide-eyed and nodded. They would have agreed to anything. But Lynda had observed the children playing respectfully with her dogs. 'They convinced her as much as we did,' says Caroline.

The Lovicks were put on the list for a female puppy. The pups would be born in a few weeks and the family could take one home when it was weaned from its mother at eight weeks old. The wait began.

The 2000 Sydney Olympics were in full swing at the time and the Lovick children, like others, were being encouraged to take an interest in them—even the local kindergarten was holding a mini Olympics. The family watched events on TV together. The children were particularly impressed by one of the female divers—Anne Montminy, a young, blonde-haired Canadian with a sunny outlook and a superb dive. They decided to call their pup Miss Montminy, or Minni for short.

Sam and Caroline took the children to see the pups when they were born, telling them they'd have to be on their best behaviour in front of Lynda. 'They were so quiet they were silent!' Caroline says.

The children gathered around the mother dog, looking in awe at the pups, wondering which one would become Miss Montminy. A little bigger than the size of a hand, the pups were squirming at her teats. Lynda allowed the children to handle them, which they did with exaggerated care. But the pups had to be returned to their mother and the children coaxed back into the car for the trip home. Excitement no longer contained, they burst into a clamour of animated observations about Grace and her family. Now the question wasn't 'Can we have a puppy?' but 'Can we have all of them?'

From then on, the new puppy was the topic of conversation at breakfast every morning.

'How long till we get her?'

'Can we go and see her in between?'

'Can we go sooner?'

'We're getting a puppy!'

Each day at school the children would write and talk about

the impending arrival of Miss Montminy in their daily 'news' bulletin.

Meanwhile Sam got down to the serious business of dog-proofing their house. He made sure the fences were secure and installed a Perspex doggie door in a rear glass wall to enable the pup to come in and out of the house as she pleased. In order to accommodate a full-grown dog, though, the flap had to be larger than usual, so big in fact that a small adult could crawl through it. An area of pebble mix was laid near the side of the house and an organic dog toilet that dissolved droppings installed next to it to help keep the area clean.

After all the preparations and much anticipation, Minni arrived, six weeks after the Olympics. The children took turns to have her sit on their laps and play tug-of-war with the soft toys Caroline bought from the op shop, making sure that she removed the eyes and other hard bits from the toys first so that Minni wouldn't choke on them. The kids took turns feeding her Weetbix in the morning, before she moved on to puppy food. The Weetbix were mixed with milk and would dry quickly in hard lumps on her fur so that Caroline had to wash her afterwards.

For Caroline, it was akin to having another baby. She suddenly had another small being to clean up after, to get into routines of naps and mealtimes, to make feel secure. Initially she put the pup in the laundry at night, which she knew was what other people with dogs did. But Minni whimpered and by the third night Caroline relented and let her out in the rear part of the house, separated from the rest of it by a 'kiddy gate' donated by friends. The next morning there were puddles everywhere; a situation that continued until Minni was toilet-trained. 'The toilet training could have been quicker if I'd been tough on her and shut her outside,' Caroline admits.

Minni was never short of attention as she continued to grow. She joined in whatever the children were doing, inside and out. Rebecca, who was five, read her *Ten Stories to Read Your Dog* over and over, played dress-ups and had tea parties with her. Rebecca painted a picture of Minni in her red collar, which Caroline framed.

But when Minni was about four months old she began to assert herself in the house, becoming more pushy around the children. She had no sense of boundaries or personal space. She would lean on three-year-old Ed and rush full speed to get to the front door if anyone was going out or coming in. Caroline imagined Minni at 50 kilos, knocking Ed over or skittling herself as she went to answer the door.

Minni needed a trainer.

7

THE TRAINER

Sam researched trainers on the internet and decided to approach US dog psychologist Wesley Laird about taking Minni in hand. Wesley lived in the Dandenong Ranges on Melbourne's fringe, where he ran an in-home dog training service.

By the time the Lovicks came to him, Wesley had had almost twenty years' experience training dogs. He had worked with every kind of dog from family pets and puppies, to movie dogs and pooches owned by Hollywood celebrities, from precious breeding and show dogs to psychologically damaged animals that no one else wanted to take on.

Wesley grew up in Pasadena, Southern California, an animal-loving boy who dreamed of becoming a vet. As a child, he'd tell anyone around him that's what he wanted to do. He was particularly fond of dogs. There'd always been a dog in his family home, among them Sandy the terrier cross, and Mercury the 'Cockapoo', as Cocker Spaniel–Poodle crosses are called in the US; they're 'Spoodles' here. But Wesley changed his mind about his career in high school after a week of work experience in a veterinary surgery.

'All the dogs that were there didn't want to be there,' he recalls. 'It was a very depressing place for me, actually!'

But the teenager had another dream—training dogs for movies. He'd watched *Rin Tin Tin* as a boy, over and over, admiring the noble German Shepherd who always saved the day; then when he was older, *The Doberman Gang*, a movie about some bank-robbing Doberman Pinschers, and *They Only Kill Their Masters*, a mystery in which an innocent Doberman is the prime suspect in the murder of its owner. Wesley was already living in the heartland of the movie industry; California is, of course, the home of Hollywood.

He was taken in by the storylines of the films he watched but, even as a young boy, he could see that the dogs were acting. He'd first realised this watching a Western movie when he noticed an animal trainer hiding behind a wagon wheel giving the starring dog its cues. Since then Wesley has never been able to watch a film with a dog in it without trying to work out where the commands are coming from. He admits he had to watch *Red Dog* several times to be able to get past this and enjoy the movie.

Although he was somewhat disillusioned to discover the 'tricks' involved, Wesley was also intrigued by how the dogs were trained to act and thought it might be fun to try it. He had a crack at training Mercury, but the family pet would just look up at him quizzically with his hang-dog eyes whenever Wesley asked him to do something new. 'I used to think he wasn't very smart but I realise now that he had pulled the wool over my eyes!' He says it is a common misconception that you can train a dog because you've grown up with one. People don't realise the work involved.

After he finished high school Wesley enrolled in a privately operated college for dog trainers where, over the next year, he learnt basic training methods. The Long Beach school was run by Steven Cobb, a strict behaviouralist who believed that everything the dog learned was by conditioning.

Wesley bought his first dog while studying, when he was eighteen; the family pets had been his brothers' dogs. He had always wanted a Doberman when he was young but his father was wary of them—the breed had a reputation for being one-man companions and fierce guard dogs. For Wesley, though, they were the ultimate in canines—intelligent, with a sleek physique and an easily managed coat. The male pup Kitaka, or Kitty, came from a breeder in Manhattan Beach, descended from a famous Doberman called Rancho Dob Storm. Wesley's father grew to love Kitty and all his son's Dobermans over the following years.

Wesley continued to study dog training even after he graduated from the dog-training college. He started working as a trainer, learning as many techniques as he could in his hours outside work. The 'Cobb method' Wesley had learnt was effective and acted as a strong framework but he was looking for a better way. 'Steven Cobb believed that dogs are completely conditioned animals—he didn't give any credit at all to the dog's natural instincts or personality,' Wesley says.

It was the early 1980s, long before the 'pack leader' concept was widely accepted and made famous by Cesar Millan, the celebrity Mexican-American dog whisperer. The theory goes that a dog's strongest desire is to follow and please the pack leader, and so the owner must become that leader. 'The worst thing in a dog's life should be a reprimand from their leader and if they know how to avoid a reprimand they'll be happy,' says Wesley.

Wesley had been interested in psychology since he learnt a little about it in high school and wondered how it could be applied to dogs. He enrolled in a child psychology class at Pasadena City College. 'There's a direct correlation, a parallel with child development and dog development mentally,' he explains. 'Dogs have the learning capacity and attention span of children of four or five years old.'

He then moved to Las Vegas where he operated kennels with two former classmates from the Steve Cobb school. The trio brought in experienced dog handlers to conduct workshops and instruct them on aspects of training, which they could then pass on to their clients. They learned techniques such as movie-set training, attack training and image training, whereby the dog acts as if it's attacking—snarling, showing its teeth, running and jumping—but all without biting. An image-trained dog doesn't bite so is safe to use on movie sets. By contrast, an attack dog that has been properly trained for personal protection is a friendly, predictable dog that will get on with anybody yet bite on command.

Image training was Wesley's 'adrenalin fix' in his twenties. He found it exhilarating having a dog lunge at him, baring its teeth and growling, knowing that the dog wasn't going to bite and that even if it did he was 'padded up'. 'There's still a primal instinct where your brain's telling you the dog's going to clamp its teeth on your arm,' he says.

Wesley would start all his clients' dogs' schooling in his kennels and then continue the training in the owners' homes, finding it more effective to teach the dog in its own territory where he could instruct the owner at the same time. 'With any type of training, it's always about training the owner more than the dog!'

At the time, the only other options available to dog owners were group obedience classes run by clubs, and kennel training, where the dog was given back to its owner after being educated. 'The more I learned, the more I realised that most dog trainers were really in the dark ages with what the dogs can do, and even with the training techniques.' Most of them were using old German obedience techniques that were at least 200 years old, Wesley says. 'We were the first to start doing in-home training.'

He undertook courses in different branches of psychology and in animal behaviour at the University of Nevada, Las Vegas, and later Pasadena City College and California State University, Los Angeles, studying part-time over twelve years. He combined his knowledge of child psychology—such as notions of 'good' and 'bad'—with what he'd discovered about animal instincts to form the basis of the methods he uses today.

Wesley's business partner in the Las Vegas kennels was keen on breeding and selling trained dogs. Wesley did likewise, even parting with Kitty. 'I always said I would only ever sell him if he'd be as happy where he was going as he'd been with me and someone would pay the price I wanted,' he says. But Wesley didn't expect anyone to pay three thousand dollars for a Doberman, even an image dog like Kitty—twice the price you'd expect to pay then. 'I cried all the way to the bank,' he quips. Then adds, seriously, 'And I cried more afterwards.'

Later he visited Kitty at his new home to do some follow-up training with his owners, a couple who were both doctors and could afford an expensive animal. Kitty now lived in a house on the beach, spending his idle hours lolling on the sand with a blonde Afghan hound. He looked content, and didn't try to follow his former owner when he left: Wesley knew he had made the right decision. He kept a daughter of Kitty's and maintained Kitty's bloodline for many years until he moved to Australia.

Wesley would hold back a couple of Doberman pups from each of the litters until they were six or seven months old then sell them with basic training, and keep some young dogs for up to eighteen months before selling them fully trained. The dogs were sent all around the US, including to a ranch in Wyoming. One even moved to Hawaii to appear on the television series *Magnum P.I.* Wesley sold another to actor William Shatner— of *Star Trek* and more recently *Boston Legal* fame—albeit indirectly; Shatner's gardener-cum-handyman picked up the pup. When the remaining pups in the litter became ill soon afterwards, Wesley contacted the owners of those that had been sold, offering to pay any vet bills for their treatment. He left a message for Shatner, who later phoned Wesley himself, thanking him for the offer. Wesley was chuffed to see the actor in a TV interview soon afterwards, holding the puppy and talking about his plans to show it.

In the late 1980s Wesley's life took an unexpected turn when he met the woman who was to become his wife, Australian TV news reporter Sally Dusting. Sally was visiting her sister in California and was working there, too. The couple married in 1992 and moved to Melbourne in March 1995, where Wesley set up a dog training business. After a friend suggested that dog wranglers and agents were in high demand in Australia, he also launched an agency, 'Dogs Only', handling animals for film sets and advertisements.

He started out doing commercials; one of the earliest being a Honda car ad that involved a Boxer looking up from a boat at a vehicle travelling across a tall bridge. The production company had been unsuccessful at shooting the ad with another Boxer that didn't like being on a boat and wouldn't respond to its owner's commands. Wesley was called in— and nailed the shot by dangling a treat from a fishing line in front of the Boxer so it would look skywards. The production company, initially sceptical about whether Wesley's wrangling would work, filmed it in one day instead of two, saving considerable expense. 'And so I became their dog guy for a while.'

More car ads followed, as well as commercials for dog food companies and for Telstra during the period that singer John Farnham was appearing in them.

One of the more complex ads was a promo for *Ground Force*, a garden renovation reality TV show on Channel Seven, which was sponsored by Pedigree dog foods. Wesley had to source seventeen dogs—all purebreds, as requested by the sponsor company—and position them in a line as they appeared to queue to see the winning property behind a velvet rope on the pavement. One of Wesley's Dobermans acted as a 'bouncer' at the doorway, with a pretty Poodle with pompom legs at the head of the queue. Wesley had to command a Boxer to come out of the house, sniff the Poodle and 'wink' at the Doberman, which would then take the rope off its hook and let the dogs inside. The wink was superimposed later, he admits. Many of the dogs, there with their owners, had been chosen for their looks rather than obedience, which made the process more complex and time-consuming. A second, easier scene of the dogs playing in the backyard was then filmed.

Wesley says he receives many calls from people who believe their pet is talented or cute. He asks them to send him photos. Half the dogs selected by production companies to appear in commercials are chosen for their looks; the other half for a special trick they can perform. And sometimes the production company wants a dog with a particular look to perform a certain trick.

Wesley's own dogs appear occasionally. Kenai, his fluffy, tricoloured Australian Shepherd, has featured in photo shoots and in three TV commercials, including a Transport Accident Commission (TAC) ad in which the owner is struck down by a car while walking the dog across the road. Kenai is filmed standing by the body of the owner, looking directly at the camera.

For another TAC ad, Wesley trained a Golden Retriever to pause in the middle of the road in front of an oncoming car that skids to a halt, causing another vehicle to career off the road and crash. The Retriever doesn't flinch as the car hurtles towards it. Wesley only sensed how dangerous a situation it could have been when the stunt co-ordinator asked him if he was wearing a belt that day—so he could grab it and pull him out of the way if the car got too close. (It didn't.) 'That was actually a fun, easy ad to do,' says Wesley, explaining that he just told the dog where its boundaries were on the road and it stayed there.

Somewhat harder was convincing a dog that wasn't particularly affectionate to put its head on the lap of an actress sitting in a car. Wesley had to get down low and hide in the car to coax the dog to reach across her lap towards him. Instructing a dog to walk into a scene and stop, while appearing natural rather than as if it's pausing for a cue, can be surprisingly difficult, too.

Wesley continued his image-dog training in Australia, directing a Rottweiler in the film *Tom White*, starring Colin Friels. The Rottweiler was filmed close-up thrusting its teeth at the lens as Wesley stood behind the cameraman. 'It was a fun game for her.' The dog, Deja, had an overbite and an oversized tongue; when she wasn't acting she would sit on the side of the set with her tongue hanging comically out of her mouth. The same dog appeared in the movie *Scooter: Secret Agent*. Other Wesley-trained dogs have appeared in *Noise*, *Three Dollars*, *Hating Alison Ashley* and *Where The Wild Things Are*.

One of his most memorable requests was to train Chinese Crested Dogs—an unusual-looking breed that is almost completely hairless—to act as aliens in a low-budget horror movie. The pampered star of the movie, a male dog, wore clothes off set to keep him warm and used to like playing with the model of himself that had been created as a stunt double.

If he was standing next to it, it was hard to pick which one was the real dog.

Throughout his many years of dog training, Wesley has seen the ugly side of dog ownership, too. He has worked with problem dogs with behavioural issues that owners have given up on, and dogs that are aggressive, many of which would otherwise have been put down. 'I know I've saved a lot of dogs' lives,' he says. 'I've never given up on a dog yet.'

When the Lovicks called him in late 2000 about Minni, Wesley had established a strong reputation in Melbourne, mostly through referrals, and had trained Giant Schnauzers before. He immediately agreed to take on Minni and the Lovicks.

The family's first lesson was about boundaries. This began with the Lovicks learning to speak to Minni in three tones of voice—a normal voice for commands, a loud harsh one for the wrong behaviour and a high-pitched 'baby talk' voice for good behaviour. Wesley explains that dogs, contrary to what a lot of people think, don't understand language and have a limited vocabulary, but they do respond to tone of voice.

Wesley put a lead on Minni, took her to the front door and taught her that standing on one side of the open door was 'good', but that crossing it without being given a release command—in this case, 'Okay'—was 'bad'. He gave Minni a sharp jerk on the lead and a firm reprimand—'Don't go!'—if she moved outside unprompted and lots of praise for good behaviour.

Then Wesley asked Sam and Ed to have a go. He showed Sam how to stand next to Ed and give Minni a corresponding hand signal as Ed gave the vocal command. 'Don't go!' Ed would say with as much authority as a three-year-old with a small voice could muster.

Minni had to understand that she was at the bottom of the pecking order. 'This dog is your best mate and she's pushing you over—you wouldn't let your best mate push you over, would you?' Wesley asked the children. He also explained that they must always be careful when correcting Minni for mistakes: 'If you tell Minni something's bad, you make sure she knows that you're not mad with her but with what she's doing wrong.'

Over the next few months Wesley took Minni and her family through his three-level training program, teaching her the basics, such as to 'sit' (remain seated until released), 'stay', 'come', walk correctly on the lead, and then off the lead, 'heel' and 'drop'. Drop is an old-school obedience training command that overrides all other instructions and can be used to keep a dog out of danger or stop it from doing something undesirable, Wesley says.

Minni was always eager to please. It was easy to teach her each step of the program and she always wanted to learn more. Wesley recalls: 'She'd show off what she'd learned before, like, "I wasn't real good at it last time but I can do it real well now!" She was very smart. I think if the Lovicks hadn't trained her, she would've trained them.'

The only thing that Minni took a while to understand was the command to drop when it was given from a distance.

Instead of dropping down where she stood, she'd walk over to Wesley first, then drop before rolling over in a submissive position, as she would do with a pack leader dog. 'It was a smart mistake—she was trying to do the right thing,' he says.

Wesley instructed the family never to use food when they were training Minni. 'You get the dog to do everything out of love for their leader. You can always show your dog approval, you don't have to always carry a treat to do that.' He adds, however, that he does use food on film sets to keep a dog motivated if he's asking it to do something unnatural or repetitive.

Consistency is important, he told the family. It was no good one person handling the dog one way and someone else doing it differently—Minni would get confused. And they had to be firm. 'Wesley's not a carrot man, he's a stick man,' says Sam.

Every day the family devoted a minimum of thirty minutes to Minni's training. Sam took dog training on as a mission. He had Minni so well-disciplined that he could take her to a field nearby and instruct her to lie down and wait at one end of it. Then he would walk to the other end of the field, blow a high-pitched dog whistle, at which Minni would run towards him, then halfway across Sam would instruct her to drop. She mastered every new request with relish. He considered training Minni for dog tracking, a competitive sport in which dogs follow scents along tracks, but had to concede that he didn't have time for the training sessions required.

Minni's formal training lasted nine months. 'Wesley had Minni eating with a knife and fork by the time he'd finished!'

says Sam jokingly. She became a trustworthy and loved member of the family, a beautifully behaved, well-balanced dog—and she needed to be for what was to follow in her young life.

8

A FATEFUL MOVE

The Lovick family had been living in their new house in Kew for fourteen months when Sam was offered a job in Boston. This required much discussion. The move would be the family's fourth international relocation and Alice and Imogen were already at school. It would involve packing up the whole household—nothing was going into storage—and, this time, there was also Minni. They couldn't go without her.

Sam's employer agreed that Minni would be relocated as part of his contract. Caroline had already planned to visit the US to see friends around the time that Sam was offered the job, so was able to look for a house to rent. She found one in Concord, not far from where they'd lived previously. It was a typical small-town American house: two storeys, with walls made of shingles, shutters, a large tree on one side of the front lawn and a US mailbox on the other side. It would suit the family, with plenty of space for the children and Minni, too. Caroline rented furniture for their new home as it would be some time before the container of their own belongings arrived.

Logistics aside, Caroline was looking forward to returning to the US and resuming the neighbourly way of life they'd led there. In Concord, you never locked your door because a neighbour might need a cup of sugar when you weren't home, Caroline explains. You might come home one day to the smell of a freshly baked cake that someone had left in the kitchen for you. And you always left your car keys in the ignition—a 'girlfriend' from down the road might need to borrow your four-wheel-drive to get through the snow. If your child fell over someone would put a bandage on its knee. Old friends in Concord were looking forward too, to the Lovicks' return.

The date when the family would fly out, and the container would be shipped, was 12 September 2001.

Two days before their departure, Caroline helped each of the children pack a small suitcase of clothes as carry-on luggage, and finished packing everything else they owned in boxes, labelled and itemised ready to be picked up and loaded into a container by the relocation company.

Everything was running to plan the day before they were due to leave. Caroline had distributed the children's school uniforms to friends. The last of their personal belongings were packed into boxes. Minni, by now almost a year old, was collected by an international pet-moving service to be taken to its depot near Tullamarine Airport. Because rabies doesn't occur in Australia, there's no quarantine for dogs departing for the US; Minni would fly out two days after the family and be picked up by Sam from Logan Airport in Boston several days after the family arrived in the States.

Caroline had trouble sleeping the night before they were due to leave and phoned her mother in England for a chat. It was not long after 11 o'clock. When her mother answered the phone, she said immediately, 'Turn on your TV but keep the volume down.'

Curious, Caroline switched on the television to witness the twin towers of the World Trade Centre in New York being destroyed, with thousands of lives lost. It was 11 September.

Caroline was soon joined by Sam in front of the TV. They watched as the chilling images of the planes ploughing through the tower walls were replayed again and again. The couple worried aloud about their friends—some commuted to New York from Concord and worked in the World Trade Centre and others had friends or family members who did. The hijacked planes had been on the flight route from Boston to Los Angeles; Caroline herself had flown on that route at least a dozen times before.

Friends and relatives in Australia and overseas started to call, worried about the family flying. 'The phone didn't stop ringing,' Caroline says. But they weren't going anywhere. All planes into and out of the US were grounded.

Caroline and Sam didn't know what to do. They couldn't go, and they couldn't stay in Melbourne; they had only the clothes in their hand luggage. Would it be safe to travel? What of their possessions? What would happen to Minni? Sam phoned the pet relocation company and arranged with them to keep her until flights resumed and she could be flown out. But the couple had to think of the children first; this was a huge disruption to their lives and they didn't want them affected by the shocking news. The family needed a distraction and somewhere to stay. So the next day Caroline booked a holiday at a resort in Port Douglas, Queensland, while they worked out their next move.

After ten days the family returned to Melbourne to catch a flight to the US—the first one bound for the States after flights resumed. The jumbo seemed little more than half full. It was a stressful flight for Caroline.

Twenty-six hours later, friends from Concord picked up the family from Logan Airport and drove them to their new home. When the Lovicks arrived, the house was unlocked, the fridge was full, the freezer stocked with their favourite ice-cream, there was a pot of homemade soup on the stove, flowers in a vase, 'Welcome Home' cards, the lights and heating were on and the beds made. Caroline was overwhelmed. 'I couldn't quite believe how beautiful they'd been,' she says.

But Concord was grieving. The father of one of Ed's kindergarten friends perished in the terrorist attacks. Caroline found herself lending black clothes to friends to wear at funerals because they either didn't own them (Americans don't favour black, as a rule, unlike Melburnians) or the shops had sold out. The funerals went on for months as body parts of the people buried in the rubble of the buildings were identified through DNA testing.

Caroline and Sam were more used to terrorism, albeit on a different scale to 9/11, than their American friends and neighbours—they'd grown up in England during a time of IRA bombings and both had experienced close shaves. Caroline was driving on the North Circular Road in London one day; she turned in one direction and a bomb exploded on the other section of road. Sam was about to board the Tube to go to work when it was stopped, along with all the other trains on the line, because there was a bomb under one of the seats. In another close call a few years later, a nail bomb exploded in Regent's Park twenty minutes before Caroline and her two eldest children were walking through it to the London Zoo. 'You looked at a rubbish bin; you thought of a bomb. But life kept going, you didn't stop.'

After September 11, though, the whole of the United States was on high alert. For Caroline and Sam, the lockdown of the US airports, followed by massively increased security, caused havoc with their relocation arrangements. The container of their belongings that was due to have landed in six to eight weeks was held up because of security concerns. In the end, it took the best part of six months to arrive; by which time the children no longer fitted into their old clothes.

Minni didn't arrive in Boston for three months. She was held at the depot in Melbourne over that time, initially due to the suspension of flights, then as regulations overseeing the transportation of animals were changed. Animals were classed as 'unaccompanied baggage', and as such, suspicious. The company Sam worked for had to pay for a veterinary assistant to accompany Minni from Australia to the US and deliver her to Sam at the airport.

A fateful move

When she arrived, Minni was emaciated and distressed. The happy puppy had gone, replaced by a frightened animal that was obsessed with food and very possessive of it. Minni no longer obeyed commands. On the first day at home in Concord, Caroline fed her then put her hand out to pat her; Minni snarled and snapped at her. Caroline was shocked. Minni had never shown so much as a hint of aggression before. Caroline wondered what had happened to her during that time she was away from them to change her behaviour so dramatically. She couldn't risk Minni biting the children yet was uncertain what to do with her.

Caroline suspected that Minni's problem concerned food and set about finding a solution.

She took every bowl in the house, and cups, too, and filled them all with dog food. There were containers of dog food in every room, on the porch and in the garden. 'The squirrels must have thought it was heaven!' Caroline says.

But it worked. After about a week Minni stopped worrying about being hungry and showed no signs of aggression. She could be trusted again.

Yet she developed another problem—she wouldn't leave Caroline's side. She would shadow her around the house, room to room, centimetres away from her the whole time. But Caroline came up with a solution for that, too. 'Right,' she told Minni, 'you're with me the whole time.'

She made sure that Minni was never left alone; if Caroline couldn't be with her, then one of the children stayed with her instead. And Minni started to relax. She became less dependent. Caroline also taught her that if she wasn't with one of the family, she could stay on a bed, which was also comforting to her.

The family took in a rescue cat—a half 'coon', the wild native American cats from Maine with no tail—that they called Mr Bingley after the wealthy suitor in Jane Austen's *Pride and Prejudice*. He kept Minni company when he wasn't roaming the neighbourhood.

It took a few months and much attention but eventually Minni recovered and became the dog she'd once been. Everything came back to her; her memories of the family, and what she was expected to do. Sit, drop, stay—she remembered every command and performed them perfectly. Food was never a problem again and Caroline gradually decreased the bowls to one bucket that always had food in it. Even today her dogs have a big shiny silver bucket of food and one of water; they feed themselves and never overeat.

Minni went on to become an 'unbelievable' dog: serene, passive, intelligent and comfortable in her own skin. Caroline adored her.

She fitted easily into their way of life, accompanying the children wherever they went or spending all day with Caroline when they were at school. Whenever Caroline visited her neighbour Sue, Minni would go, too. Sue had a son, James, who was the same age as Ed, and a Beagle called Ruby, and the dogs and boys would all play. The women also walked together with their hounds, sometimes twice a day. Minni befriended the local mailman, too, jumping into his van and riding down from the Lovicks' house to Sue's with him. Ruby, though, would take one look at the man approaching the family's letterbox and chase him. After she'd bitten the mailman one too many times, Sue's mail was suspended and she had to collect it from the post office until she promised to keep the biting Beagle under control. In winter, when there was snow on the ground and walking wasn't a pleasant proposition, the Lovicks would exercise Minni by standing at their front door at night with a torch, shining it down the street and round in loops as Minni ecstatically chased it.

Three years later in mid-2004, Sam was wooed by a company in Melbourne to be their chief economist. It was an irresistible offer. And as much as the family loved their life at Concord, they were keen to go home. So the Lovicks prepared to move again.

As soon as Caroline knew that they were leaving, she researched what was needed for a 'dog passport'—she didn't want anything to hold up Minni from going back with them. She learned that to gain the passport the dog had to have a number of injections, within a strict timeframe, and have them documented. So Minni was given single shots for diseases including rabies and distemper, so the results would be clear-cut. When Minni was completely up to date with her vaccinations, Caroline arranged for her to see a government quarantine vet for a full physical examination to clear her paperwork. The vet told Caroline he wanted to double-up on Minni's rabies injection, as it was due to expire while she was in quarantine in Australia, but when he gave her the injection he administered a triple antigen that covered rabies, distemper and antibodies for leptospirosis, a disease spread by bacteria that can be fatal. Dogs with leptospirosis antibodies in their blood, which they get from these shots (as well as an infection) are banned from Australia. 'And that was it,' says Caroline.

When the vet realised his mistake, he declared Minni positive for leptospirosis on her paperwork as she now carried the antibodies in her blood.

'Her blood count will go down soon,' he reassured Caroline. 'Then we'll ship her out.'

It was July 2004; the Lovicks were due to leave in two weeks. Minni's antibody level did not go down.

Just days before they were due to leave, Caroline, by now distressed, was thrown a lifeline. Sue offered to look after Minni at her home until she could be cleared by the vet to be sent to Melbourne. She would take her for the blood tests, and, most importantly, Minni would be with people she trusted and who could look after her properly. Caroline was sure Minni was in good hands but it was still heartbreaking to leave her behind on 31 July. She consoled herself with the thought that it wouldn't be long before Minni re-joined them.

Minni went to the vet for blood tests every fortnight and every fortnight the tests were positive. The antibody levels in her system varied wildly but there were no indications that they'd come down. Ironically, she was never going to contract the disease because she'd been immunised. The situation dragged on, and one day in late October, Caroline was talking with Sue on the phone when Sue mentioned that James was having problems at school. He'd really clicked with Minni, who was sleeping on his bed, she said. Caroline felt her heart sinking.

Meanwhile, Sam had also been talking to Sue's husband Jack about the dog.

'I think Sue wants to keep Minni,' Jack had said. Sam thought about this, but avoided discussing it with Caroline.

A fateful move

It was three days before Christmas. Minni's antibodies were through the roof. Sam and Jack spoke again and decided that it was best for Minni to stay with Sue and Jack's family. The situation wasn't going to resolve itself, they decided. Minni could be spared the trauma of quarantine and was happy where she was.

'I don't know how I'll tell Caroline,' Sam said.

Caroline was devastated. It had been painfully difficult to leave Minni behind; now there was no hope of having her back. The children, who'd been missing her too, were very upset. Minni had been the family's first dog, a constant presence in their lives, and best friend.

Caroline has been to the US several times to visit friends, including Sue, since the move to Melbourne in 2004. Each time she visited, Minni would run between her two 'mummies' making sure she gave each of them attention.

Minni lived with Sue for the rest of her life and died in 2013, at the ripe old age of fourteen.

Caroline still keeps a photo of Minni on her mobile phone, which she looks at lovingly from time to time.

9

AN UNUSUAL ABODE

Sam had visited Australia in July 2004 to find the family a house to rent, again looking for a property in Kew. He soon phoned Caroline to say he'd found just the ticket—a spacious two-storey, red-brick house with enough bedrooms for them all, in a good location near the secondary schools the children would attend. And it was secure. *Very* secure. The house was surrounded by high brick walls with gates, had security surveillance cameras, deadlocks on doors and even a steel grid that could be locked at the top of the stairs that separated the ground and first floors.

Lease signed, Sam caught up with friends Alan and Harriet Nelson, who also lived in Kew, and whose children Tom and Jack were friends with the Lovick children. Sam, Alan and

Tom were out riding bicycles around Kew together one day when Sam yelled out, 'Come on, I'll show you where the new house is!' They pedalled into the street and as they neared the address, Tom suddenly stopped.

'No—it can't be this house!' he said.

Sam confirmed that it was.

'Oh my God, you've rented The Murder House!' Tom said.

Sam turned to look at his friend's son. He had no idea what Tom was talking about.

'That was Graham Kinniburgh's house,' Tom explained. 'You know, he was killed outside it.'

Sam hadn't heard of the grisly event in the suburb's history because the Lovicks had been living in the US when it occurred. Graham 'The Munster' Kinniburgh was an organised-crime figure, one of the most influential gangsters in Victoria, if not Australia. He'd lived in the house for fifteen years before being gunned down in front of it in a gangland-style killing on 13 December 2003.

'Oh, for God's sake, don't tell Caroline—she'll never move into it!' Sam said.

The family moved into what became known as 'The Murder House' in late August.

Caroline was immediately uneasy. The children had started back at school, leaving her alone in the cavernous abode. She was without the familiar things that usually surrounded them, which were still en route in the container. And she had no dog.

The phone would ring and when she answered, the caller would hang up. Strangers loitered outside the front gate. She would see cars pausing outside the gate. None of the neighbours talked to her.

The Lovicks changed the phone number and started locking the gate at all times. Whenever they went out, Caroline would lock the children in the car in the garage, reverse out, then lock the garage again. She'd moved from small-town America where everyone kept their doors open to a suburban fortress.

The police dropped in once to see how Caroline was, which gave her some comfort—they'd had the house under surveillance on and off for years. But with Sam regularly travelling for work and the children at school, Caroline frequently found herself at home alone and anxious.

As the year ground towards Christmas, she missed Minni terribly. She sensed that Minni wasn't coming home, although that decision was yet to be made, and knew she had to move on from her. In the week before Christmas, Caroline marshalled the family into the car on the pretence of buying a charity Christmas tree. The RSPCA in Burwood sold them as fundraisers, she said. On their way to Burwood the family passed several outlets selling Christmas trees—and each time they did the children howled and asked why they couldn't just stop and get one there.

Sam, who'd grown up with four cats, picked the first kitten, a 'weird little cat' at the back of the pen. In the tradition of Mr Bingley, the coon cat, he was named 'Fitz' after Fitzwilliam Darcy, hero of Jane Austen's *Pride and Prejudice*. The children chose Kitty, a small grey tabby, named after one of the Bennett sisters in the same book. Back home the frisky kittens took everyone's mind off the Murder House and Minni—almost.

Around the same time Sam called Lynda Tyzack. He knew that Caroline really wanted another dog—one like Minni.

'I need a pup,' Sam told Lynda. 'What are the chances?' Unfortunately Lynda didn't have any pups then, nor were there any on the way.

Christmas, New Year and most of January 2005 passed by and Sam was in the US for work when Lynda called the Lovicks to tell Caroline she had a young dog in desperate need of a new home. She had only four days left before she had to get rid of him. 'You met Ralf at the show last year,' Lynda said.

Caroline recalled that the Lovicks had seen Lynda and Jenny Moore with two dogs, one of them a handsome six-month-old pup, at the Royal Melbourne Agricultural Show in September, just after they returned from the US.

'He's got a barking problem,' Lynda warned. 'And he's a *big* dog.'

'Yes, absolutely, we'll have him!' said Caroline.

It was a confluence of events that would ultimately bring joy to hundreds of people.

10

HAVOC

'I've got my giant! I've got my giant!' Caroline exclaimed, as she watched Lynda lead Ralf along the wharf at Station Pier in Port Melbourne. Ten-year-old Rebecca, who had also risen early to watch the *Spirit of Tasmania* dock at six o'clock, looked expectant, too excited at the sight of the dog approaching them to be embarrassed by her over-exuberant mother.

Lynda and Ralf had travelled overnight; Ralf below deck in a crate in the hold, Lynda in a cabin. The young dog had taken it all in his stride, having crossed the Tasman before with Lynda and Jenny to compete in the Royal Melbourne Show. The staff were, however, as cautious as ever, insisting that Lynda take Ralf off the ferry first, before the other passengers, and standing well back as she led him out of the crate.

As Lynda walked Ralf along the wharf, the passengers stood around the sides of the ferry, watching. Some pointed and made comments about the dog, the likes of which they'd never seen before. Jet black, all muscle, with a burly chest and powerful hindquarters, Ralf was the size of a small pony.

As they drew closer Caroline turned to Rebecca and said to her, almost under her breath, 'I just don't remember him being that *big.*'

'Ralf coming Saturday' was all the text message said that Sam received from his wife that week. Sam, in the US for work, glanced at the message and wondered momentarily who Ralf was. The Lovick children, though, *had* been briefed about the new dog they would soon get—a re-homed hound with a behavioural problem—and were looking forward to Ralf's arrival. They were expecting Ralf in the same way that you might expect, say, a naughty cousin.

But as the time drew closer, Caroline worried what Sam would think of her executive decision about their next pet. Sam had asked Lynda for a puppy; Caroline had agreed to a dog in his absence, and what turned out to be a rather sizeable one. 'What have I done?' she wondered. She reassured herself that despite Ralf's barking problem—and any other unruly behaviour he might have—he was one of Lynda's dogs and bred to have a wonderful temperament. Ralf was coming to a home that was big on training so the family could act on his behaviour, and if all else failed they could always try those Citronella scent anti-barking collars, Caroline told herself.

Meanwhile Lynda had her own concerns about how Ralf would adapt to living with a family—even though the Lovick kids were experienced with dogs, he'd only occasionally met children at shows and wasn't used to them. Children can sometimes unnerve animals with their unpredictable movements or screaming, and she knew that some dogs didn't cope.

Sam had just returned from the airport when Caroline, Rebecca, Lynda and Ralf walked in. 'Whoa, he's not like Minni!' he said. Ralf was a third the size of Minni again, and bolder. But the four children were soon all over him and Caroline knew that whatever reservations her husband had about Ralf, he'd give him a fair go; Sam was, after all, a soft touch. Lynda and Caroline sat and chatted over tea and toast as they observed—on the overhead security monitors—Ralf exploring his new environment, nosing his way around the rooms of the house. The four children followed him around but looked disappointed as he turned his attention towards their two kittens—Ralf had never seen a cat before. The two women stopped talking for a few moments as they waited to see what he would do. Ralf maintained a respectful distance from the kittens, sat and watched them.

Lynda stayed at the Lovicks' house, which struck her as being big, dark and strangely gloomy, for a couple of hours to make sure that Ralf was settling in. Despite their initial concerns, he'd been on his best behaviour while she was there, and had behaved perfectly with the children. She left happily, thinking 'Ralf will be fine'.

Ralf was, as Caroline predicted, unerringly good-natured. He was also completely unaware of how to live within a family household. He'd previously lived in the company of other dogs with a single adult owner. He had no idea of his place in this new pack. On that first day Caroline watched horrified as Ralf approached the children when they were eating, and took the sandwiches out of their hands and ate them. He was gentle but saw no reason why he shouldn't do it. He didn't seem to understand the meaning of 'no'. He didn't respect personal space, and simply pushed the children around as needed.

Within hours of welcoming their new dog, Sam was on the phone to Wesley Laird.

One of the first things Ralf did when no one was looking was to remove the rolls of toilet paper from their holders and drag them round the house. The house had three toilets, so there was toilet paper everywhere—lengths of it trailing through rooms, shredded piles all over the floor. 'You'd go to the loo and there was never a roll there,' says Caroline.

Ralf would look up genially and seem somewhat confused as Caroline scolded him. He knew what was at the centre of those rolls and that it was meant to be played with. *What do you mean I can't take them?*

He trashed the kitchen bin, tipping its contents all over the floor in his search for food. He raided the pantry and stole potatoes, onions, flour, almonds, raisins, sugar—anything that was edible, even if barely. He'd take out the rolls of foil and plastic wrap to play with. Ralf's saving grace was that he didn't chew—the socks he'd steal from bedrooms were found intact, if soggy, after he carried them out. Caroline could always tell which child hadn't been picking up their clothes by the size of sock Ralf produced.

A week after he arrived Ralf perpetrated his most egregious misdemeanour.

The Lovicks were hosting a dinner party for Sam's brother-in-law Peter who was visiting from England. The table was set for twelve people and Sam was about to carve a large fillet of beef he had left on the kitchen bench when Ralf stood up on his back legs, picked the beef off the bench and made off with it. He'd got halfway through the kitchen towards the dining room when Sam roared at him and he dropped it.

'Sam put it back on the chopping board, carved it up and we ate it!' admits Caroline.

The guests thought it was funny, although one of them remonstrated theatrically when offered a second serving of beef.

Ralf took his admonishment with good grace but the incident established the pecking order in the household—Sam, in Ralf's mind, had just become top dog.

Wesley Laird arrived that week at the Lovick's to meet an overexcited and out-of-control Ralf that jumped on people, wouldn't sit and appeared anxious about what was expected of him. Wesley immediately told the family that Ralf needed to be taken back to the early stages of training, to learn about boundaries. 'And you're going to have to establish these boundaries very quickly,' he warned.

Wesley had trained show dogs before and knew where Ralf was coming from. 'Most show dogs aren't taught to sit because in a show ring when you come to a halt, the dog has to stand,' he explains. 'I've met a lot of people who are under the impression that you should not obedience-train show dogs—that it takes down a dog's spirit.'

Ralf responded well to his first obedience lesson. He learned quickly that he wasn't to go out of the house without a release command. The Lovicks remembered the methods from training Minni, so knew what to do and were consistent with Ralf. The puppy silliness soon subsided.

By the end of the second lesson, he had become almost *too* relaxed. Whereas Minni was eager to show off what she'd learned, Ralf would do the absolute minimum required. 'He's definitely a character!' says Wesley. 'He had the attitude that he'd do as little as he had to do—but no more,' he says.

At the end of that session he said, bemused, to Caroline and Sam, 'Well, you can train him and he'll do it when you ask him today but he might not do it next week!'

Wesley explained that Ralf was a great dog but needed to settle down. 'And you need to be stronger with him,' he said. 'If you cut him too much slack, he'll take advantage of it.' He told the children that if Ralf was going to have any leftovers, they must always put the food in his bucket rather than hand it to him until he learnt some manners. As he left that day, he assured the family that it wouldn't take too much to train Ralf: 'You know what the commands are. Just put in the time. You can do it!'

The Lovicks and Ralf took so well to the training—Ralf being an older puppy and the family knowing what they were doing—that they were able to progress through Wesley's program in three lessons. Within a fortnight, Ralf knew what was expected of him—his place was at the bottom of his new pack.

Says Wesley, 'Once they showed they were committed to him—that he was part of their pack and was there to stay—he relaxed.'

Throughout the time they trained Ralf, Caroline started to observe some of his idiosyncracies. She recognised that Ralf, though obedient, would always do everything in his own time. When he was asked to do something, he'd glance at her as if to say, 'Yeah, in a minute,' or give her a questioning look, 'Are you sure you want me to do that? Oh, alright.' But she also started to glimpse another side to him—a softness, a gentleness, a *knowingness* that would set Ralf apart as being special.

Over time, Ralf's training helped curb his behaviour around food—but he was still obsessed with it.

In the first few months after he arrived, Caroline was buying a new bin every couple of weeks as he demolished the previous one in search of food. He once helped himself to meat she was thawing in the sink (for his evening meal, mind you), standing with his front paws on the bench, heaving it out and spiriting it away.

But the family started to see progress. After a while Caroline and Sam could safely leave the Sunday joint on the kitchen bench, confident that it would not become Ralf's lunch, though he was still happy to consume the remnants of the children's school lunches—an uneaten cheese sandwich or a bread roll—taken from the bins in their bedrooms.

Ralf learnt to refine his techniques. Now he uses the power of persuasion. When Caroline puts out bowls of sweets and chocolates for the children and their friends, he sticks limpet-like to anyone who takes one, or even looks like they might. Under his mournful gaze, few can resist passing him a treat. (Unlike many dogs, Ralf's not allergic to chocolate and can eat it without falling ill.) He shows the same undivided attention to anyone eating cake, almonds, pistachios, peanuts or tomatoes.

He eats chewing gum—with the wrapper on. Often this misdemeanour is only detected when the foil comes out the other end and is noticed in the garden. The same thing happens with Easter eggs, only the clue then is coloured foil.

Caroline recognised early on that behind his spirited behaviour Ralf lacked confidence. He wee'd on the floor sometimes when Sam reprimanded him then slunk off to one of the children's rooms to be comforted. The two kittens dominated him, lying on him as he lay on the floor, digging into him with their claws, ruling him in a way that was embarrassing, Caroline says. He didn't find his bark at the Lovick house for six months.

Ralf also had a terror of confined spaces. Caroline tried locking him in the laundry at night when he first arrived, but he panicked, furiously scratching and pounding at the door until he dislodged it from its runners and got out. Ralf slept on one of the children's beds from then on. One morning during his first fortnight, he somehow locked himself in the bathroom while Caroline was taking the children to school—and tore up the bottom part of the bathroom door in his attempt to get out. On another occasion he broke the lower part of a side gate when the family went out.

So Caroline started taking Ralf out with her. She took him to the cafe, to her friends' houses, the hairdresser, shopping—everywhere that Caroline went, Ralf went, too. And so they began to form a deep bond.

For a dog whose main outings had been to shows, Ralf was unusually relaxed about being taken out onto streets full of distractions and with cars whizzing past. Nothing frightened or worried him. He wandered around amiably, stopping to greet every person, enjoying the attention he invariably attracted.

Most of all, he adored going to school. Caroline would walk him there and back every day, with Rebecca and Edward on either side of him. He would say hello to every person and every other dog on the way. Once he got to the school grounds, he'd wait as all the pupils filed through the gate and wouldn't leave until the school bell rang. After school, he'd be swamped by children wanting to pat him. And when it came time to go home, Caroline had to drag him away. He braced his paws on the ground then dropped to the pavement and became a dead weight. Caroline hauled at the lead, attempting to shift him while trying not to look embarrassed.

Ralf, it emerged, just loved children, *any* children.

11

A RETURN TO
THE SHOW RING

After a year, the Lovicks moved out of the Murder House into a home elsewhere in Kew. Caroline was relieved—she'd always felt unnerved living there. The house had never ceased to be a source of curiosity to people. Strangers still walked or drove past, looking in. Parents she knew from school would drop their children off for play dates and ask if they could come inside for a look. Caroline would take them on tours. She recalls the time she and her friend Harriet decided that there must have been a stash of loot hidden somewhere and, like characters in a Nancy Drew mystery, searched the garage. They didn't find anything, but it helped to have a sense of humour about it.

Happily for Ralf, the new home had a backyard—whereas the

previous one only had an enclosed courtyard—and a swimming pool. Harriet's family had a pool and Ralf had learnt to swim there with the children. It took him a little while to get the hang of it, though—his rear end was so heavy that it sank. Once he'd mastered dog paddle, he took to swimming around collecting leaves, later picking them out of the pool on request.

Ralf also enjoyed catching birds in the backyard, carefully carrying them inside in his mouth, wings folded, fluttering but unharmed, to give to the family. He'd put the bird on the floor, looking proud of himself, then leave whoever was home at the time to try to get it outside again. He was enthralled by the ducklings Alice brought home from school as part of a science project; he stared transfixed as they waddled along and watched as they swam around the kitchen sink, standing on his back legs with his front paws on the bench and trying to lick their heads.

In mid-2005, the Lovicks were surprised to receive a call from Lynda, asking if they would allow her to enter Ralf in the Royal Melbourne Show in September. Ralf would be eighteen months old and eligible for the junior dog category.

Caroline thought it would be fun to see Ralf compete so agreed—as long as Lynda handled him in the ring. Lynda, and her Miniature Schnauzer, who was also entered in the show, would stay with the Lovicks and help them prepare Ralf the day before.

On the morning before the show Caroline and Imogen helped make over Ralf for his return to the show ring, washing him in black shampoo, dyeing his coat to disguise any hairs that weren't jet black then plucking out any white hairs they'd missed with tweezers. *I can't believe I'm doing this*, thought Caroline as she plucked.

Lynda neatened his eyebrows, trimmed his beard and clipped his face and the area beneath his tail. Ralf stood quietly as they tidied him, as if remembering what showing was all about.

Caroline worried, though, as they arrived with Ralf at the showgrounds, that he would let Lynda down, disgrace her as a dog breeder and exhibitor. By now he was a family pet, used to lying around, seeking out people to pat him, rolling around on his back on the floor. He looked beautiful and moved well but Ralf could easily decide to sit or lie down in the ring if he felt like it. Caroline wondered how Lynda would get him to pay enough attention to behave like a show dog.

From the moment Lynda led him into the ring, Ralf was his endearing self, looking around for someone to pat him, including the other dogs' owners and the judge. While the other dogs looked aloof, Ralf looked completely relaxed, Caroline says. When he was inspected and called out as a finalist, he looked like he was thoroughly enjoying the attention the judge was according him. But Ralf paraded like he knew what he was doing. He came second. Caroline would have been chuffed had Ralf won but she wasn't worried that he didn't—she believes that dog shows should have a behaviour component, that the competing dogs should demonstrate that they're well socialised with other animals and with people. Besides which, there was another chance for victory.

A return to the show ring

As is often the case with dog shows, the organisers of breed societies try to hold their own events close to the time of the Royal Melbourne Show when all the competitors are in town. So the following day, Ralf was entered in the Schnauzer Club of Victoria show held at KCC Park in Skye, the state's epicentre for doggie activities. But the plans came unstuck when Lynda tripped at the Royal Melbourne and twisted her ankle. Her foot swelled up like a balloon. She asked Caroline if she would exhibit Ralf instead but Caroline knew that Ralf would be too playful and focus on her rather than what he was meant to be doing.

So Caroline came up with another solution: 'Sam, you're going to show Ralf tomorrow!'

Ever up for a new challenge, Sam agreed. He'd seen the movie *Best in Show*—a comedy about the ultra-competitive world of dog showing—surely it couldn't be that hard? *Why not?* he thought, *You can fake it!*

The next day he donned a brown sports jacket with matching shoes, shirt and tie, and a pair of freshly ironed chinos—cream-coloured to act as a backdrop to Ralf's immaculate black coat, and drove, bemused, with Caroline and Imogen to KCC Park. The Lovicks met up with Lynda in a huge building that looked like an aircraft hangar, where Lynda gave Sam a crash-course on some of the techniques he'd need to show Ralf to best advantage. Lynda took one look at Ralf's lead, shook her head and replaced it with a leather-handled show leash with a fine metal chain. She instructed Sam on how to hold the chain up high and short above Ralf's neck to keep his head up, how to stand him so that his back legs splayed out, his nose was in the air and tail up. Owners are allowed to hold the tail up, Lynda said, but Sam tried and Ralf's tail went *down* whenever he touched it so he decided to ditch that idea. Next was how to run the dog on the lead, making it stride out and show off its gait—too slow and the dog looks frumpy, too fast and it looks a shambles.

As he waited for his event, Sam observed how cloistered the show dogs were; if they weren't being groomed, they were locked in crates before they competed, then as soon as they'd finished they were whisked away into the owners' cars. 'The owners are terribly touchy about dogs at shows—you can't get near them,' he says. It was such a serious business, he reflected, and there was money involved—a puppy related to the Best Dog in Show can be sold at a premium.

Ralf's class was announced and his little entourage made its way to the ring. Imogen, the family photographer, found a good position on the side of the ring to record the event, but Caroline hid at the back of the rows of spectators with Lynda so that Ralf wouldn't see her and become distracted.

Sam and Ralf, and the other competitors, assembled in numerical order outside the ring. Sam glanced around at their rivals as they moved off. He knew the dog to beat was Goofy. Goofy, or Refrain All Star, was a famous show dog imported from Finland. Goofy lived in Brisbane but was blitzing shows around Australia at the time. He was Number One Giant Schnauzer in Australia in 2005, 2006 and 2007, breaking the records set previously by one of the Ritzau family's foundation dogs. Goofy's handler wore a smart white suit. Lynda, meanwhile, took one look at him coming into the ring and thought 'Oh no!' She hoped that his elephantine ears (as she liked to think of them) would count against him but had to admit to herself that he looked as good as ever. As Sam cast his eyes over him, he thought, 'That dog is so *Best in Show*.'

But he also knew that Ralf was a fine example of the breed. Ralf, he told himself, clearly had the best muscle definition—'the Arnold Schwarzenegger of the show ring. It's because of all the exercise we give him.'

Sam found himself warming to the occasion. Showing Ralf was actually fun. Not taking the protocols of showing overly seriously, he chatted to the judge as she inspected Ralf, thinking it was interesting that she'd travelled from Israel for the event. The judge was happy to have a conversation, too, as she went about her business. Sam was confident as she inspected Ralf's mouth—'Ralf's got great teeth,' he says—but less sure as she felt his coat. That was his worst fault—not as wiry as was desirable. Ralf's ears no longer stuck out as much as they did when he was a pup so they weren't the conformational problem they'd once been.

The judge called out the finalists, Ralf among them, and asked Sam to run him around. Ralf had been trained well when he was young and moved with an expressive spring to his gait. Sam, by now thoroughly enjoying himself, as good as pranced along with him. Then it was decision time. The finalists lined up before the judge and stood expectantly. Caroline, who had been 'laughing like a drain' as she watched her husband trot around the ring, squeezed her eyes closed and crossed her fingers. The winner was Goofy.

It wasn't the end for Sam and Ralf, though. They still had the Australian-bred class to compete in and, with no imported Goofy, they were a good chance. Sam repeated the performance, feeling like an old hand by now. This time, they won.

Ralf was judged Best Australian-bred Schnauzer. Caroline gave a little cheer.

Sam and Ralf were reunited with Caroline and Imogen after the event and posed for photos with their blue rosette. Lynda was thrilled for the Lovicks and also for Jenny Moore, back in Tasmania, whose faith in Ralf as a show dog had been vindicated.

But that was the end of Ralf's show career.

'We're done,' said Sam, as they left. 'We're just not show dog people.'

Ralf's career as a show dog ended there but something happened at the Royal Melbourne that made Caroline sense that he was destined for another even better future.

Ralf was different to other dogs at the shows. Most handlers have a strict 'hands-off' policy when it comes to people wanting to touch their dogs but the Lovicks allowed Ralf to be patted by anyone who asked.

While most of the other dogs were kept in cubicles in the dog pavilion at the Melbourne showground, as the public walked up and down the aisles looking in at them, Caroline and Lynda waited between events on their fold-up chairs with Ralf lying on the ground between them. Ralf was patted throughout the day, and he relished it.

There was one encounter Caroline would never forget. A couple pushing a pram down the walkway between the rows of cubicles slowed down to look at Ralf, when their little girl suddenly clambered out of the pram and flung herself onto him, hugging him tightly and refusing to let go. The parents panicked but Caroline stepped in quickly. 'It's alright—my kids do that to him all the time,' she said.

Although the parents didn't mention it, it appeared to Caroline that their daughter had Asperger's syndrome—she noticed that the youngster didn't make eye contact and looked down at the ground as Caroline tried to talk to her. But the girl was obsessed by Ralf, pulling his hair playfully, touching him all over the face, banging the top of his head with her palm. 'Ralf melted like a marshmallow,' says Caroline. He seemed to know that the pummelling and pulling was just her way of showing him attention. The girl's mother was in tears as she watched on.

Eventually the little girl switched off Ralf, and her parents took the opportunity to say their goodbyes, thanking Caroline, and her dog. Caroline never saw the couple and their daughter again, but somehow one of the organisers at the show heard of the incident. Three months later, Caroline received a message from a woman from Dogs Victoria, the peak body for pure-breds in the state. Dogs Victoria (also called the Victorian Canine Association) brings together a wide range of dog activities, including showing and sports. It also runs a therapy dog program that oversees volunteers who visit aged-care and other institutions with their pets.

The woman told Caroline that she'd heard the story of Ralf and the little girl at the Royal Melbourne, explained about the therapy program and ended by saying, 'We think your dog would make a good therapy dog.' The organisation was holding a training program to start in March the following year—would Caroline consider it?

Volunteering is something both Caroline and Sam's families valued and believe is important for everyone to do. Caroline shook tins for World Vision and Oxfam as a teenager, and sang carols for charity. As an adult she helped out at the kindergartens and schools of her children, and their Scout and Girl Guide groups. She acted as a volunteer advocate for families and children with special needs. She's done so much volunteering, in fact, that Sam once had a T-shirt printed for her that reads 'For God's sake stop me before I volunteer again!' So when Caroline was presented with the chance to take part in the dog therapy program, she jumped at it, pleased at the prospect of the work it would lead to—and at the novel idea that she could do it with Ralf.

And with that decision, Ralf found his real vocation in life.

But before he could take that path, there was the matter of his love life to be sorted out . . .

Ralf is one of these pups, in Ulverstone, Tasmania.

Ralf, still technically a pup, competing at the Launceston Dog Show with Jenny Moore.

Lynda Tyzack putting Ralf through his paces at the Royal Melbourne Show, September 2005.

Ralf placed second in the Royal Melbourne Show's junior dog category.

Bird-loving Ralf when he was about eighteen months old.

Ed with Minni and Bingley the cat in Concord, Massachusetts, in 2001.

Sam Lovick prepping Ralf for his appearance at the Schnauzer Club show in 2005.

Caroline and Ralf in the Lovicks' backyard.

Trainer Wesley Laird, who worked with Ralf, overseeing a TV commercial.

Ralf (left) with daughter Ivy in August 2007.

Ivy gives her father a playful scruffle, early 2009.

The Lovicks (from top left): Edward, Rebecca, Sam, Caroline, Alice, Ralf, Imogen and Ivy, late 2011.

The two dogs, pool-side. Ralf is on the right.

Ralf enjoys an occasional dip, even if his bottom sinks.

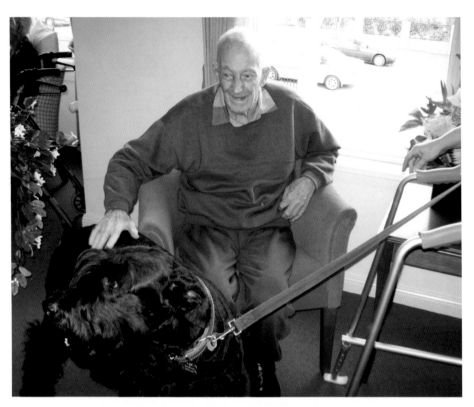

Doug Tanner, one of Ralf's favourite elders at Trinity Manor.

Carl, the resident dog at Trinity Manor, a charmer by all accounts.

12

MARRIAGE AND FATHERHOOD

Harriet Nelson was a born-and-bred Boxer woman until she met her first Giant Schnauzer. Her family in England owned Boxers from the time she was born and throughout her child-hood, and Harriet then had a succession of Boxers herself, ending, by the time she was married with two children, with Molly. She didn't know that Giant Schnauzers existed before her friend Caroline asked if she'd go with her to help pick a puppy. She met Minni at Lynda Tyzack's home and thought she was 'absolutely gorgeous'.

Harriet, a willowy blonde who spoke with well-rounded vowels, investigated the possibility of buying a Giant Schnau-zer herself in mid-2004. Molly was getting old and she thought that introducing a pup into the house might give her a new lease on life and be great company. She went to a large dog show in Cranbourne and met a breeder from Sydney who, after much negotiating over the following fortnight—'she was unbelievably protective about her dogs'—agreed to let her buy a pup from the latest litter. In September 2004, Harriet flew to Sydney to make her selection. 'Lulu' was four months old and had an impeccable pedigree on both sides—her mother Zena was a multiple times Best In Show winner, a 'multi-BIS' in dog-showing parlance, and her father was the record-breaking Goofy.

Molly did perk up when Harriet introduced her to the new member of the family, becoming livelier in her movements and even teaching Lulu to 'box' with her front paws. 'Molly was quite ancient then, but she started to look like a younger dog,' says Harriet. Sadly though, the Boxer died six months later.

About the time that Harriet bought Lulu, the Lovicks arrived back from the US and moved into the Murder House. Caroline, who was missing Minni, would come around to Harriet's house to smooch Lulu, adopting her as her surrogate dog for a while. She recommended that Harriet call in Wesley Laird to train the pup early. Wesley did such a good job of establishing boundaries with Lulu—within minutes—that when Harriet's brother-in-law once tried to take Lulu for a walk when the family wasn't home, she refused to move past the front gate. 'Wouldn't budge,' Harriet says, laughing. After unsuccessfully trying to drag her, he had to carry her out. 'There's something wrong with your dog,' he told Harriet when she arrived home later.

When Lulu met Ralf in the courtyard of the Murder House not long after he arrived at the Lovicks, it was love at first sight, says Harriet. Ralf was a handsome young buck, a big boof who was 'full of himself', she recalls. The two young dogs played together well, and from then on saw each other whenever Caroline and Harriet met, and when the children from the two families were together. Both families later had swimming pools, and the dogs loved them—the pair of Giant Schnauzers would take a flying leap into the water together as soon as the pool gate was open.

It didn't escape the Lovick children's attention that Lulu was a girl and Ralf a boy and there followed much pestering for a litter of pups. Caroline and Harriet eventually relented and agreed that the dogs could have a litter together and that the Lovicks could pick one to keep. 'You want a puppy, you take responsibility for it,' Caroline warned the children.

But they didn't stop there. The dogs had to get married first, they insisted. And it had to be a proper wedding—with rings, vows, a vicar, bridesmaids and wedding outfits. The ceremony was held on the lawn of the Lovicks' backyard. Lulu wore white with a veil attached to her collar draped over her head. Ralf sported a blue homemade bowtie, matching his best man, who was Edward. A friend of Rebecca's officiated as the vicar and one of the girls was Lulu's bridesmaid. As Ralf waited for her, Lulu made her way down an aisle (a path made of beach towels) past the congregation sitting on either side of it.

'I couldn't believe we were doing it,' says Caroline. 'But the kids nailed it!'

Harriet swears that Lulu and Ralf sat down after they had been pronounced 'dog and wife', turned to each other and touched noses. Caroline noticed it, too. The dogs were relieved from their matrimonial duties after the vows and scampered away to rip Lulu's veil off, caper on the lawn and eat cupcakes.

Then it was just a matter of waiting for Lulu to come in heat and picking the right time in her cycle. The first attempt was unsuccessful; Ralf wanted to mate, Lulu just wanted to play and snapped at him when he tried to mount her. So they tried again later. Caroline brought Ralf to Harriet's house when the children weren't home and they left the dogs to it. It didn't take long before Ralf mounted Lulu but they stayed there locked together for what seemed like a long ten minutes. Caroline and Harriet worried to each other that they might have become *stuck*. It was a stressful business to watch; the women had to have a glass of wine afterwards to calm their nerves.

Lulu grew 'fatter', as the children observed, and barely two months later her belly was swinging down towards her ankles. She gave up swimming and when the family went on a holiday to the beach she would stand in the shallows looking longingly out to where she would otherwise have swum.

The first puppy, a female called Charlie, was born at five o'clock in the morning of 2 January 2007, weighing 330 grams—big for a pup. Harriet discovered the newborn pup with its mother on the wicker couch outside, Lulu's favourite spot to lie. Harriet moved them both into a large cardboard box, which had been prepared for the birthing.

Harriet's children, Tom and Jack, looked on amazed as each slippery little pure black sac popped out, the pups bleating as

Lulu released them and licked them clean then nuzzled them towards a teat. An hour after they were born, the pups were dry and sleek. Harriet tied a different-coloured ribbon around the neck of each one so she could tell which pup was which. The Lovicks were summoned to watch more pups being born later that day. They'd left before the eleventh puppy emerged stillborn at three in the afternoon. The day had been hot and as Lulu finished giving birth, with a last heave and pant, she stood up and staggered over to the pool to sit on the steps and cool off.

When the pups were three weeks old, Harriet left her husband, taking the two boys, ten pups and Lulu with her to a rental house. The house fortuitously had a garden shed, which became the dogs' home until they were old enough to be sold. The rear garden had a raised lawn where the pups would play—and occasionally roll over the edge as they did. If one of the children went out to lie on the lawn, they'd soon be covered by a swarm of biting and licking pups. Harriet says they were a wonderful distraction at a difficult time. 'Having just left my husband, it gave us all something to do and kept us all together. It was a great experience.'

But also an exhausting one. There was a huge amount of work involved in caring for the litter. Lulu couldn't feed all the pups herself because there were so many of them, so Harriet had to bottle-feed them and clean up after them. By ten weeks old they were already big, the size of an adult Beagle. The backyard would sometimes be a frenzy of furry black bodies. The puppies played havoc with the garden and chewed the irrigation system. Harriet lost her rental bond when they moved out.

Caroline brought Ralf—who was spayed not long after he consummated his 'marriage' with Lulu—around to see his offspring when they were a few weeks old. He took fatherhood in his stride, sniffing the pups once over then ignoring them— he was more excited to see Lulu again. The Lovicks visited again when the pups were five weeks old to pick one, which they would later collect to take home. Harriet had already picked Charlie for her family. She'd been told that if you wanted to keep one pup from the litter that would be living with its mother, you should pick the one that the bitch went to most often, and that was Charlie. The Lovicks chose Ivy, a female born in the middle of the litter.

Harriet says that whenever the four dogs are together now as adults, Ivy still defers to her mother and Charlie to Ralf. The two sisters go 'ballistic' whenever they see each other and play like they don't play with other dogs. Ralf and Lulu are still drawn to each other like magnets. The four of them playing in a park are quite a sight, so overexcited as a pack that Ivy once bowled over Caroline in her exuberance.

Harriet sold most of the pups when they were between eight and ten weeks old, minding one of them until it was four months old for the new owners who were on their honeymoon. The pups were quickly snapped up: 'I could have sold them a hundred times over,' she says. Most went to breeders or show homes, though Harriet never followed their progress as show dogs. Charlie was a pin-up girl for the Royal Guide Dogs Calendar 2007, which featured dogs other than working guide dogs. Ivy auditioned, too, but missed out, while Charlie became Miss October.

Harriet remarried seven years later, telling her new beloved when they started dating that he would have to learn to love her Giant Schnauzers 'or we won't be a couple'. He does.

Caroline occasionally finds herself telling people she meets on her volunteer rounds about Ralf's wedding, the story of the dog that got married enthralling young patients. The Lovicks themselves occasionally look back on the event with a chuckle, aware that to anyone listening Ralf could be mistaken for a real groom. Indeed, they sometimes have to remind them-selves that their treasured family member is in fact, a dog.

13

ALONG CAME
IVY

Two-month-old Ivy settled in well with the Lovick family, getting only the occasional look from her father for behaviour he didn't approve of and learning quickly to bark in unison with him. Arriving as a pup, she had to accept that her place was the lowest in the household's pecking order. 'There's the cats at the top, then us, Ralf then Ivy,' Sam jokes.

The household was a busy, lively place, with constant comings and goings; Ed, in Year 5, was playing hockey after school; Rebecca, in her last year of primary school, was rehearsing for a tap and jazz show; fifteen-year-old Imogen was often out kayaking; and Alice, in Year 12, went to singing practice on top of her studies and social life.

By the time Ivy came along, the Lovicks were well-versed in

dog training so took her through Wesley's lessons themselves. After a while it would only take the pointing of a finger from Caroline for Ivy to do as she was asked.

The two dogs always had a bucket of dry food available if they were hungry but Ivy was often open to a forbidden snack. Consuming untended cat food was a particular favourite, and was also one of Ralf's few indiscretions; Ralf would bolt down the first few mouthfuls before Ivy snuck off with the ceramic bowl, taking it outside to finish the contents. Miraculously she never broke the bowl.

Guileless Ivy raided the larder sometimes while the family was out—a crime that was instantly detected. Instead of rushing to the door to greet the family as she usually did, Ivy would sulk, hang-dog, in a corner, tail between her legs. But Ivy just *looks* guilty whether she is or not. You only have to hold up an empty bowl and say 'What's this?' to Ivy and she'll look shame-faced. Ralf could be caught with his paws on the bench eating something, turn and look at you briefly, then keep chomping.

The dogs would help themselves to the pears from the tree outside the back door—ripe or not—springing up to reach the fruit on higher branches after they'd harvested the lower ones. They ate the mint from Caroline's herb garden, too, although their palates don't run to Vietnamese mint. Ivy ate the chillies. But the garden, unlike the kitchen, is their domain; it's fair game.

Remarkably, neither dog has become ill after eating something they shouldn't have, although Ivy had to be rushed to the vet one morning when Caroline found her curled up and unwilling to greet her. Ivy's stomach was bloated, as hard as a coconut. It was peak hour in the household, the children finishing breakfast and getting ready for school.

'Go now, take her to the vet,' said Sam. 'I'll drive the kids to school.'

Caroline bundled Ivy into the wagon and wove her way through the busy morning traffic to the vet's surgery as quickly as possible. The whole time Caroline feared the worst—she'd heard there'd been dogs in the neighbourhood that had been poisoned before burglaries were committed. Caroline and Ivy were immediately shown into an examination room, where she explained that her pet had seemed well the night before yet had become bloated and uncomfortable that morning for no apparent reason.

But as the vet began to examine her, Ivy started farting. Odorous blasts of foul wind filled the surgery. No treatment was needed.

'I think it might have been the pumpkin,' said Caroline.

The dogs knew what to do if asked but were always allowed a certain amount of leeway and the occasional spoiling, as is often the way with family pets. 'But when I mean it, they do it!' says Caroline. There's one rule that's absolute—no jumping. A dog the size of Ralf jumping up on people is dangerous. When Caroline was accidentally knocked over in the park by Ivy, who weighs 40 kilos, it took her a good week to recover; she'd fallen hard on her back and was badly winded.

After a while, even Wesley Laird's edict that dogs should only be fed in their bowls was occasionally breached. 'You know, we were never going to feed our dogs at the table,' says Caroline. 'But we do.'

The dogs do have table manners, though. They sit quietly next to the family, never drool and refrain from pestering for food, although Ivy gives the nearest leg the occasional nudge. Every now and then someone smuggles a morsel of dinner under the table and into one of the waiting mouths. Even Caroline occasionally slips food to Ralf under the table, her daughters say, although she strenuously denies it when caught. Sam lets Ralf lick his bowl after he's finished his ice-cream, and whenever Caroline makes a slow-cooked casserole she puts the leftovers in the ceramic cooker on the floor for the dogs to polish off before it goes in the dishwasher. 'It's the pre-rinse stage,' she says. 'I don't know what people do without dogs! Though I suppose people who don't have dogs would look at us and be absolutely appalled!' she adds, happily.

Ivy learnt to swim early on, and she and Ralf often enjoy a dip together. At the mention of "wimming' they bound to the back door, skidding and tumbling on their sides on the wooden floorboards and slate tiles as they scramble to reach the dog flap and the pool. On a few occasions they've cracked the glass on the wall around the perspex door in their mad rush to get in or out, and the Lovicks have had to replace the whole pane. The dogs will play in the pool for hours, chasing a hollow metal ball around with their noses, trying to grasp it; when they eventually puncture the ball, the Lovicks have to buy another.

After their swim, the dogs come inside for a warm shower and shampoo. 'It's Pantene,' says Caroline, 'costs us a fortune!' The dogs are towel-dried in the kids' bathroom or blow-dried by one of the family if they need to be ready to go somewhere in a hurry, a process Ralf enjoys, blissfully closing his eyes and swaying his head this way and that as the warm current of air moves over him.

As Ivy grew up, it emerged that she had a quite different personality to her father. She is livelier—she's the one who stands on the lounge chair to bark frenetically at approaching visitors, and who gets overexcited and sweeps things off the coffee table with her tail. (Ralf's tail was docked when he was a pup before the practice was banned, so he doesn't do this.) Ivy's a princess, says Caroline, she likes to be noticed. Ralf is less demonstrative. If he gets excited his hind leg quivers. When he gets extra excited—if he's particularly looking forward to a member of the family coming home or is offered an extra big chewy treat—his teeth chatter. Ralf is usually placid though and appears to understand what's going on around him. 'He reads peoples' feelings,' says Sam, 'Ivy just wants to play.'

Ralf senses when any of the family are ill, staying by their bedside, pacing around, then lying as close to them as he can get. He was on Ed's bed constantly when Ed broke his leg playing sport in Year 9. 'You know instantly when one of the kids is ill—Ralf's on their bed before they've even got a temperature,' says Caroline. 'He picks it up even when I haven't.'

Ivy is overwhelmingly affectionate. She wants to be patted constantly, nudging you under the arm if you're sitting on the couch not paying her enough attention. She frets if the family are away. Ivy can be heard whimpering if she thinks she's been left at home by herself. And she's an emotional eater, says Rebecca. If Ivy was left long enough by herself she'd take a loaf of bread from the pantry and eat it, leaving only the plastic bag. After several stern reprimands from Sam she stopped eating the loaves, but she'd still compulsively take one if she were alone, dropping it on the kitchen floor or leaving it in the backyard when she suddenly realised what she'd done.

Ivy lost her confidence with other dogs after she was bailed up by a German Shepherd-cross when she was young. The dog had seen her in the park and unprovoked ran headlong towards her, knocked her over and pinned her to the ground with its jaws on her neck. No blood was drawn but it scarred Ivy psychologically for life. While she behaves with other dogs in public most of the time, she will occasionally switch into defence mode at the sight of an unknown dog and has to be steered away.

Ralf, too, was attacked on a walk once but shrugged off the incident. He and Caroline were strolling in their local park when a Jack Russell spotted him, slipped his collar and lead, ran up to Ralf, took a flying leap at his flank and latched onto it with his jaw. As the diminutive mutt hung off Ralf's side by his teeth, Caroline turned to his owner and said, 'Would you mind getting your dog off mine, please?' The owner prised the Jack Russell off and Ralf issued a low grumble, his only protest. The man flinched, picked up his dog and without so much as a word, headed off. Caroline took Ralf home to bathe his punctured side in disinfectant. She says that despite the number of people who scoop their little dogs off the ground and cling to them as Ralf passes, it's usually the small dogs that have a go at the larger ones.

There are other differences between the dogs, too. Ralf's partial to watching television; Ivy appears not to notice it. He particularly enjoys *Animal Planet*, a documentary series, and positions himself in front of the screen when the program is on, edging up closer to it as the animals appear. He becomes almost puppyish as he watches, his stump of a tail wagging furiously. He growls whenever a ferocious, snarling wild animal appears. He likes, too, the animal segment of *Australia's Funniest Home Videos*, barking whenever there are pets involved in the antics. Occasionally he'll go round to the back of the television to look for whatever's on the screen. The Lovicks tried muting the sound to see if Ralf was responding to that but he wasn't. He'll look closely if anyone points out that 'there's a doggie on TV'. Yet Ivy's smart. She worked out how to open the pantry doors when the Lovicks thought they'd succeeded in locking the dogs out. If they really want to stop Ivy from raiding the food they have to loop a tea towel through the cupboard handles and tie it off with a double knot. 'She likes a challenge!' says Caroline.

Ralf and Ivy are important members of the Lovick household but they're not like extra children, says Caroline. The dogs are more like best friends. 'They're always happy to see you and they always say yes, right up there with a bestie! Kids are quite judgmental—they'll say, "You're not going out in *that*, are you?" A dog will think, "You're going out in that T-shirt, great, come on, let's go!"'

14

BOMBPROOFING RALF

It was a weeknight in March 2006, after dark and cold by the time Caroline and Ralf arrived at KCC Park for the first weekly session of the Dogs Victoria therapy dog course. Fourteen or so people of all ages milled around at one end of the vast indoor pavilion with their dogs, a variety of breeds, all keen to get going. There was a sense of camaraderie in the group, the feeling that everyone was there because they wanted to see their canine companions well-trained and helping others. A man and woman appeared without dogs: instructors who would guide the group in the months ahead.

After welcoming everyone, the instructors told the gathering what was expected of the dogs and owners. The owners were to use a collar, instead of a chain leash, and told that the dogs would be expected to be under control on a loose lead at all times; their attention focused on their owner and what they were doing rather than the dog across the pavilion from them. They were then split into groups of four or five and taken through some basic training to check that the dogs were obeying their owners.

After a few weeks, the instructors began to introduce new exercises, such as getting the owners to walk their dogs around chairs. The dogs were expected to weave their way in and out of the chairs without touching them, learning an awareness of their bodies and how to negotiate tight spaces. Doing the course was like climbing a staircase, says Caroline, each week a new step taken slowly and with care.

The dog owners were asked to come to a weekend intensive course, held in a classroom, during which they learned what they could expect while working as volunteers in various institutions. They were taught about privacy and respecting the space of those they'd visit, and cautioned that, while they might be dog lovers themselves, not everybody appreciated a close encounter with a canine.

The instructors then progressively began introducing some distractions, such as the sight of a wheelchair, then a person in the wheelchair, then the person in the wheelchair approaching the dog, then later brushing against them with it. Some of the other dogs baulked at the sight of the chair, others barked at its wheels. Ralf looked at it as if to say, *So what?*

The dogs were exposed to all kinds of sounds; whistling noises, the hissing sound made by a bike pump, sudden loud noises, banging. They were allowed to react to the noises at first, but were expected to learn to ignore them. All sorts of medical trolleys and drip stands were wheeled past them.

The instructors watched the dogs closely at every stage to see how they reacted, and that no dog was uncomfortable with the training, marking their progress throughout the course. Some of the dogs couldn't get past a particular stage and dropped out. Ralf, though, didn't react negatively to any of the experiences in any of the stages.

'It was so well organised and managed,' says Caroline. 'All along the message was, "We're not going to upset your dog".'

The course spanned over a year, culminating on a day when the dogs and owners were tested—exposed to all the experiences in one session. Ralf cruised through the test and graduated with a Therapy Dog Certificate on 21 August 2007.

The months of training had paid off but there was another course to complete before Ralf could work with children: Promoting Responsible Dog Ownership training would prepare him to go into schools and kindergartens. This course acclimatised dogs to classrooms and the behaviour of children, using adults pretending to be children—in case any of the dogs bit them. Children can be unpredictable and move quickly, meaning that anything that goes wrong happens swiftly. Dogs graduating from this course had to be bombproof.

Again, Ralf completed the program without a mark against his name, doing whatever was asked of him in his usual affable way. Caroline wasn't worried about the final testing day, scheduled for 21 November, and expected that Ralf would cruise through this as he had done before.

But only days before, Imogen was diagnosed with an abscess above her eye and needed urgent eye surgery. The operation was scheduled for the day before Ralf's test. Caroline was torn; she wanted to pick her daughter up from the hospital after the operation and look after her, but Ralf had to attend the test day to be accredited.

Imogen, like the rest of the family, had followed Ralf's progress throughout the course, and was aware of her mother's commitment to having him fully trained as a therapy dog. 'He just has to go for the test,' she told Caroline.

Yet there were moments during the test when Caroline almost wished he hadn't.

The final trial for the Promoting Responsible Dog Owner-ship course was held at a property at Oaklands, near Tulla-marine Airport, a series of buildings that reminded Caroline of an old air force base, with neatly kept garden beds, lawns and connecting footpaths.

The atmosphere was decidedly formal. The owners had to register, provide identification to prove who they were and submit their police-check documents. Their course instruc-tors were present but took no part in the process, which was conducted by the examiners, men and women in uniform shirts.

The examiners explained that the owners would be asked to take their dogs through a variety of scenarios—classrooms, playgrounds, a mock hospital and busy sidewalks among them. Some of them would be confronting, they said. Not everyone would pass. The dogs that did had to be perfect. Caroline listened intently, starting to get nervous; Ralf was almost asleep on the floor.

The dogs and owners were then broken up into small groups, which would rotate around the different scenarios. Caroline was directed outside with Ralf. In the first test, a man rode a bike past Ralf so closely that Ralf had to shift quickly sideways to avoid being hit by its pedal. He was mugged by people, acting as a crowd. They pulled on Ralf's beard and stubby tail. They stood lightly on his toes, poked and prodded him.

Caroline was stunned. She hadn't expected this. She choked up as she watched Ralf endure the tests and was upset with herself that she was putting him through it. Ralf submitted willingly to it all.

Inside, there were more challenges. Adults pretended to be children in a classroom. 'Pick me! Pick me! Pick me!' they screamed at the 'teacher'. Another room was set up to resemble a hospital; another an aged care home, with wheelchairs and people walking slowly in frames and shuffling around using walking sticks. Volunteers mimicked the appearance and voices of the elderly, patting the dog with a shaking hand, speaking in an exaggeratedly loud tone as a person who was hard of hearing would do. 'HERE, DOGGIE, HERE DOGGIE, HERE!' Some simulated the voices of people who speak slowly and awkwardly or in a slightly guttural way, as might people with acquired brain injuries.

The examiners watched closely the way the dogs approached people, how they sat with them, their reactions to being patted on the top of their heads and to having their ears pulled. They scrutinised the dogs' body language—any behaviour that suggested a dog was shy or stressed, and the owner would be stopped and asked to re-present the dog later. A large, noisy trolley was wheeled past Ralf, brushing his side as it did. Ralf ignored it. Caroline noticed other dogs shying away from the clattering trolley. Even when a smaller tea trolley loaded with food appeared, Ralf took no notice.

Back outside again, Ralf was bumped by a wheelchair and then pushed over onto the ground. Caroline winced as an examiner fired an air pistol next to Ralf's ear just as a low-flying plane roared overhead. Ralf didn't so much as flinch.

'Wow!' the examiner said. 'Does he react to *anything*?'

'No,' Caroline replied, before remembering the mad dash for the pool that the mention of ''wimming' brought on.

She was relieved when Ralf finished his last scenario. He'd done everything that was asked of him, confidently and calmly.

'He's amazing!' said one of the examiners.

'Bombproof. Fantastic,' said another.

Caroline looked down at Ralf and felt proud. The test had been tough—it no longer exists in that form—but she knew that Ralf was now prepared for any situation that could be thrown at him. He'd done, as she puts it, the Rolls Royce of therapy training.

They weren't through yet though. While Ralf was taken for a walk outside by one of the instructors, Caroline was called into an office for an interview to discuss what she and Ralf would be doing as volunteers. The man who interviewed her praised Ralf then proceeded to ask Caroline how committed she was to the idea of volunteering. 'Do you have time to devote to it?', 'Are you prepared to travel?', 'Can you do it regularly?' were among the questions he asked.

Caroline assured him that she'd already considered all of the requirements and discussed them with her family.

'Great!' he said, and shook Caroline's hand. 'Welcome aboard.' He then went through some logistics with Caroline, writing down her size for a volunteer's T-shirt and the size of Ralf's collar. And then he said, 'And you'll be issued with a computer to take into the classroom with a presentation on it.'

Caroline's heart skipped a beat. 'But I don't do computers,' she said.

The interviewer looked at her quizzically.

Caroline explained that she prefers old-fashioned communication, a legacy of her dyslexia. She thinks fast, so is good at verbal communication such as debating a point, and with anything spatial, but not with the written word. It would be difficult for her if computers were crucial to the program. But she didn't like the idea too of using a pre-recorded presentation rather than demonstrating what needed to be conveyed with Ralf. 'If you've got a dog in the room, why are we looking at a computer? This might be the first dog the children have ever handled,' she says. Caroline considered the matter briefly at the time and told the man she'd have to think about it.

She went home with Ralf and thought about it further but felt the same way still; she rang Dogs Victoria a few days later to say thanks but she wasn't interested in that program.

It was a setback but not one that was going to affect Caroline Lovick for more than a few minutes. 'Life always hands you something,' she says.

15

WORKING THE MANOR

'Ralf was one of those lovely, well-behaved dogs I wish everybody had,' says Nicky Abell, the woman who gave him his first assignment. It was early 2008, but she still recalls him vividly: 'He had this gentle expression. His good soul would shine out of his face.'

Nicky, the long-term organiser of Dogs Victoria's therapy dog program, phoned Caroline not long after the training test at Oaklands to say that a nursing home in Balwyn, close to where Caroline lived, was keen to have a therapy dog visit regularly. He'd respond well to the people at Trinity Manor, she said. Large dogs such as Ralf can cope better with someone with impaired motor skills and shaky hands because they are solid and stable. And because he is so tall, he could sit next to a chair or a bed of anyone who was immobilised and be within reach. 'Would you be interested?' she asked Caroline.

Ralf's first day as a therapy dog at Trinity Manor began with a word that would come to excite him as much as the mention of a walk or a swim: 'Working'.

'You're working today, Ralfie, you're going to have to be a good boy,' said Caroline, as she clipped the lead to his collar and led him to the car. She'd been briefed beforehand about what to expect on her first day at Trinity Manor, a family-owned aged care home that prided itself on a high standard of specialised residential and rehabilitation facilities, including dementia, respite and palliative care.

Caroline parked in the tree-lined street outside the two-storey building as Ralf looked expectantly out the window. She felt conspicuous as she and Ralf made their way past the paved semicircular drive with its central garden and fountain, and through the entrance, Ralf's nails tapping on the polished ceramic-tiled floor as they approached reception. But in the foyer she was welcomed warmly by Julie Rankin, then Trinity's Lifestyle Coordinator, and Nicky Abell, who were going to accompany her and Ralf on their first day.

They started on the ground floor, walking into a communal area where a group of 'elders', as they are called, sat in comfortable lounge chairs beneath an overhead TV, walking frames and wheelchairs at their sides. One or two had nodded off, chins on their chest. As they entered the area, the residents looked up at them, some nudging each other, their faces animated, a mixture of shock, awe and delight at the sight of the unusual visitor. Several people laughed.

'This is Caroline,' Julie said, 'and her dog Ralf. They're going to come in to visit.'

'Goodness gracious,' said one elderly lady. 'He's big!'

'My word,' said the gentleman to her side. 'He must eat an awful lot.'

And then a series of questions that Caroline would be asked many times over in the years ahead: What sort of dog is he? How old is he? How much does he weigh? How much does he eat? Where does he sleep? Caroline would always answer the questions enthusiastically, as if it were the first time she'd ever been asked them.

As Ralf stood by her side, waiting to be allowed to go up to the group, his back leg started quivering—the tell-tale sign that he was excited. After a few minutes, he was allowed to approach one man, and immediately put his head on the man's knees then slid down slowly on his front paws until he was lying on his feet, leaning into him. He would do this often afterwards, offering warm, close comfort.

Ralf remained snuggled into the man's feet as Caroline chatted to the group. Then he turned his attention to a woman who was vigorously motioning to him to come over. She leaned over and took his head in her hands, carrying on a long one-sided conversation with him, fussing over his eyebrows and the hair on the top of his head, oblivious to all around her but Ralf who was looking up at her intently. Anyone else who was interested was accorded the same devoted attention. When all the residents in the lounge had had a pat, Ralf and Caroline went on to the next communal area. It was a routine that they'd come to know well.

Trinity Manor is a cheery, gracious place. Its tasteful last-century décor wouldn't look out of place in many of the houses in the well-to-do suburb; framed artworks in the cream-coloured corridors, decorative cornices, pelmets over tasteful drapes, classic lampshades and floral arrangements on side tables. Every now and then a 'quiet area' opens to a courtyard garden or balcony where people can rest and reminisce. There are kitchenettes for the residents to make themselves and their visitors a cup of tea or coffee and a café downstairs for those who like their coffee brewed.

Caroline met elders who were conversational and computer savvy in areas where they could socialise, watch television or Skype their friends and relatives. She encountered others else-where who were silent, wrapped up in worlds of their own. In the high-dementia area, several residents sat at a table engaged in therapeutic activities using shapes and colours, designed to stretch their cognitive and creative abilities. Caroline was shown the hairdresser's room where Ralf would later sit while an elder had a trim or a perm. About the only place he didn't go was the gym.

When invited, Caroline and Ralf went into the elders' rooms—personal places decorated with possessions that spoke of their lives. Photos of family, a favourite piece of furniture, a crocheted bedspread, a painting they had created themselves, treasured pieces of china or a vase, photos or models of cars. A woman with Down's Syndrome had on display a trophy she won as an athlete competing in a regional event in the Special Olympics in Victoria. Many had a radio by the bed, often playing opera or classical music, and a whiteboard for reminders about visitors, past or future, medical appointments and events at Trinity Manor.

Caroline caught glimpses of long lives richly lived. As she was admiring one man's beautifully handcrafted rocking chair, she learned that he was a photographer who'd travelled the world for decades, beginning his travels before World War Two. 'He was taking photos before I was born,' says Caroline. 'He must have a phenomenal archive but he talked about travelling the world as if it was popping out to go to the shops in Kew.' That man, Doug Tanner, was to become one of Ralf's favourite friends at Trinity.

With paws the size of saucers, Ralf would clamber onto the beds when invited, and settle in; the elders would squeal with laughter. They touched his beard and felt his ears. Some of the women tried brushing his fringe out of the way so that he could see better. One added a bit of saliva on her fingertips then smoothed Ralf's fur back the way you would straighten a child's wayward lock of hair. Sometimes Caroline would take an elder's hand and guide it towards the velvety hairs on Ralf's muzzle; the person would turn their head towards her, look up and smile.

Some elders wanted to feed Ralf but he had been trained not to accept food from hands so Caroline would ask them to put it on the arm of their chair for him. Sometimes the residents had a son or daughter with them; seeing Ralf for the first time, they noted his size, drew breath and wondered if he would bite. Later those same family members would insist that Ralf visit their parent: 'Oh, *Ralf's* here today, Mum!'

Caroline greeted all the residents cheerfully, chatting with them in her singsong English voice. An effervescent bright-eyed woman, she engages warmly with everyone she meets and makes them feel as if they've known her for years. She would visit once a fortnight on Wednesdays, spending at least five minutes, and up to forty-five minutes, with each of the fifty or so elders at Trinity Manor, talking about whatever came to mind. But, she says, 'I might as well have been invisible!' They were always focused on Ralf.

After a while a visit from Ralf once a fortnight wasn't enough for the elders. Caroline and Ralf, who could stay for up to six hours at time on their Wednesday round, frequently returned the day afterwards, too, if someone had missed out because they were sleeping during Ralf's visit or had a doctor or physiotherapist's appointment. 'My problem is that I can't say no!' Caroline jokes.

In March 2009, Jessie Bainbridge took over as Lifestyle Coordinator of Trinity Manor and accompanied Caroline on her visits—and soon became one of Ralf's biggest fans. Jessie recalls the way Ralf walked around like 'a lazy prowling lion', moving languidly through the corridors, his head turning from side to side to see what was going on, looking for all the world like he owned the place.

Jessie would sometimes phone Caroline on days other than Wednesdays if one of the residents was having a bad day or was worried about something. She and Caroline would take Ralf over to the distressed person and he'd cock his head to one side and look at them as if to say, 'So what's going on?' He'd sit down next to them and they'd instantly relax. 'It was like flicking a switch,' says Jessie. 'Nothing fazed that dog.'

Trinity Manor upholds what's called the Eden model of care, which maintains that life for elders is about continuing to grow and thrive, with the help of others. It's about countering loneliness, helplessness and boredom by fostering a rich and diverse daily life in a community of residents. There are planned outings, a visit to a country pub, perhaps, and annual events such as Anzac Day ceremonies. There's also a 'sensory garden' courtyard with herbs, fruit trees, fragrant flowers and the soothing sounds of running water. There are quiet leafy corners to rest and contemplate. Aromatherapy. Floral arrangements everywhere. A calming yellow and blue colour scheme. Music wafts out from various rooms, whether it be old-time, war-time, the Beatles or the Seekers. Groups of local school or kindergarten children visit regularly.

Therapy dogs aren't the only animals to visit. Special days are arranged when farm animals are brought in for elders and their relatives to touch, smell and feel. Every Easter, an incubator is set up where chicks hatch from eggs and grow for a week—always a favourite with grandchildren or great-grandchildren. Ralf didn't bat an eyelid at any of the other animals he encountered there—cats, dogs, rabbits, birds, calves and pigs among them.

Jessie says that Trinity Manor is well aware of the benefits of pet therapy. 'It calms people down and lifts their mood if they're depressed. The more animals, the less the usage of antidepressant drugs. The families also see the therapeutic benefits—the happiness and euphoria that can break a depressive moment.'

Before she began the therapy-dog work, Caroline knew that she needed to be mentally prepared for all kinds of behaviour: people who have brain tumours, for instance, could be even-tempered one week then belligerent the next. People with Alzheimer's often have what's called Sundowners Syndrome where they become anxious, and sometimes agitated, as the day goes on. But more often than not, Caroline and Ralf were greeted by warmth and gentleness. As the months went by, she came to know personally the elders and their ways.

She speaks fondly of a married couple who would sit in the same spot in the first floor lounge in the morning of Ralf's visiting day, looking out the window, waiting for him to arrive. Ralf had his routine—Caroline says she often felt like she was just following him around—and the couple would be the first people he'd visit. The wife gave him pats and kisses, the husband would feed Ralf sections of mandarin and grapes. Ralf developed his liking for fruit at Trinity Manor. The couple celebrated their sixtieth wedding anniversary there, although they slept in separate rooms as the husband needed more intensive nursing care. They could remember few other appointments except that 'Wednesday is Ralf's day', Jessie says.

Caroline came in one week to find the husband lying unresponsive, seemingly unconscious. She talked to him as Ralf rested his nose on the man's bed. Perhaps he could hear her. She talked some more. Ralf waited. The man's face was calm, his body still. But Caroline noticed that his fingers were moving—slowly, up and down on Ralf's face. He died not long afterwards.

Ralf had other favourites, too. One woman always greeted him as her 'handsome man'. And then there were the people who gave him food. Some elders would put a bit of their afternoon tea aside for him and he remembered who they were. He also knew who dropped their food and would do a quick vacuum around their chair as he visited.

Caroline and Ralf occasionally joined the large gatherings held in the all-purpose room. A spacious communal area with a donated piano, it is often used for concerts, during which an elderly gent might spontaneously rise to his feet as a melody sounds, seek the hand of a lady, and waltz. Taking Ralf into a room where the staff were holding other activities was always a risk, though, says Jessie: 'Ralf upstaged us all.'

During the training program, Caroline often had been reminded that not everyone loved dogs, and was taught how to deal with this, so she was always respectful of residents who didn't fully embrace their canine visitor. One country woman, perhaps more used to having working dogs outside, was happy to have her bed lowered so that she could pat Ralf's head. 'He's a lovely dog,' she said as she stroked, 'but I don't believe in dogs being inside!'

Ralf and Caroline's visits usually went without incident but they once approached a room where a woman took one look at Ralf in the doorway and shrieked. Jessie quickly asked Caroline to take Ralf out of sight. She explained that the woman was a new resident with dementia. She'd been a vibrant, independent soul earlier in life and was having trouble accepting that she needed care. 'Get out of here! What are you doing here? Leave me alone!' she would shout at Jessie.

'People with dementia are often angry and frightened when their routine is upset and when they find themselves in a new environment,' Jessie explains.

They respected the woman's privacy and let her settle in. A few weeks later, though, Jessie thought about trying Ralf again.

'I have a friend, Caroline, who has a therapy dog, Ralf. Do I have your permission for them to visit you?' she asked.

'Alright then,' the woman snapped.

Later that day Caroline and Ralf visited the woman. Ralf immediately sat down and put his head on her lap. The woman started caressing his head. 'Babuschka, Babuschka,' she crooned. Then she broke into a broad smile—the first time Jessie had seen her smile since she arrived—and laughed. It was the breakthrough that Jessie had been hoping for.

Jessie talked to the woman's son the next time he visited and told him, 'I saw the most beautiful smile on your mother's face the other day when Ralf was in.'

'Yes, I've heard all about Ralf,' said the son. 'Who is he?'

'He's four-legged!' said Jessie, explaining that Ralf was a therapy dog.

The son looked surprised. 'But Mum doesn't like animals,' he said, smiling and shaking his head.

'He thought it was brilliant,' says Jessie.

Another woman in her eighties was non-communicative. She wouldn't walk, either, and would sit all day with her hands firmly clasped on her lap, refusing to undo them. Yet each time

Ralf appeared, she would suddenly exclaim 'Oh Ralf!' and let loose a stream of chatter and laughter as she cuddled him. Three minutes later she'd be catatonic again. 'I wish I could bottle those moments,' says Jessie. For the woman's relatives, witnessing them was a bittersweet experience.

Jessie and the other staff would call Ralf in when they needed his help in other difficult situations. One woman with dementia refused to get out of bed. When Ralf came visiting she would become animated, slap the bed with her hand and say, 'Up! Up!' Ralf would climb up and stretch full-length beside the woman as she buried her head in his hair. Then, one Wednesday afternoon when Ralf was due to come in, Jessie reminded her that Ralf would be in the building soon. 'He can come up on the bed with me,' the elder piped up.

'No, he's only downstairs today,' said Jessie. 'If you want to see him, you'll have to go there.'

The woman agreed to get out of bed and allowed herself to be helped downstairs to see Ralf. From that day on she was happy to go to wherever Ralf was—and she would talk to people as she went.

Another resident in his late eighties could be particularly bad tempered, yet when Jessie asked him to help her out by accompanying Ralf on some of his visits, he happily took on the task. 'Ordinarily he would have said, "No way! I'm not here to work for you!" But it gave him a purpose, a job to do, and that was very satisfying for him,' says Jessie.

'Ralf brought out the best in people.'

As well as lifting emotions, therapy animals like Ralf provide physical benefits for the people they visit. Elders who sat rigidly in their chairs for hours on end and made minimal movements would bend forward to pat him, forgetting their aches or ailments, stretching their backs as they did it. The staff were surprised to see residents they'd noted in reports as 'not moving', and who physiotherapists couldn't convince to move, suddenly bend or lean forward to touch Ralf.

Petting Ralf would sometimes spark memories for an elder of being a child and having a dog, or a friend or neighbour having a dog. The staff listened to their remembrances and learnt a little more each time about the elders' lives. Ralf not only reminded some of them of their childhood pet, sometimes he *became* their childhood pet. He was Ralf for a while then a dog with another name thereafter. A French woman, who was bedridden, enjoyed having him on her bed with her, giggling as he joined her. In her more lucid days she'd tell Caroline about the dog she'd owned when she was young, a German Shepherd. As the visits went on she lost the capacity to speak in English and spoke to Ralf in French. 'He wasn't Ralf any more, he was "Puschka",' says Caroline.

One woman with Alzheimer's loved Ralf when she first met him then one day burst out yelling, 'Get that dog out of here! . . . If Dad sees it . . . Get that dog out!' She was back in her childhood and Ralf was a family dog that was in danger.

A blind woman whose family had given up her guide dog took a little solace in the surrogate pet but still wept when Ralf was there, pining for the loss of her own best friend.

The staff at Trinity Manor enjoyed the sight of the canine visitor, too, though it took some of them time to get used to

Ralf. Several who were from countries where dogs are feared and not kept as pets were hesitant about getting too close to the big black animal. One staff member told Jessie she wanted to touch Ralf but was too scared. Jessie suggested that the woman stand behind and put her arms around her, then stretch out to pat Ralf. With a roomful of people watching, the woman grabbed Jessie around the waist and peered over her shoulder at Ralf as they inched towards him. She stretched out to touch Ralf as he extended his nose to sniff her hand. Everyone laughed with her, cheered her on and clapped.

Yet Ralf wasn't the only dog at Trinity Manor. One man had brought his own dog, Carl, to live with him. Professor Ian McDonald, a renowned cardiologist, had adopted the Jack Russell–Dachshund–cross as a young homeless dog and now shared his room with him. Carl accompanied his owner in his motorised chair on walks to the local park, where he was popular with the other dog owners. Carl was somewhat stout despite his regular exercise—he wasn't allowed into the dining room at meal-times but would wait outside until he heard the clink of plates being removed from the tables and then helped clean up food from the floor. There were members of staff who refused to go into the room with Carl at first, but once they worked out that he was harmless they were soon taking photos of him on their mobile phones, sending them to friends and relatives in their home countries, whether Indonesia, India or China.

Carl adored Ralf. The two dogs would lie on the bed with their noses together and play in the adjoining courtyard. Professor McDonald delighted in watching them. Carl would bring his ball out for Ralf but he took no cheek from his large buddy, his somewhat doting owner says.

The residents' families are also encouraged to bring in their pets when they visit; Pomeranian, Maltese and Shih Tzu dogs have all visited, and Patterson the rabbit. A volunteer who helped with carpet bowls brought in her two Border Collies. Sherly Narikuzhy, who co-owns Trinity Manor with her husband George, brings in her German Shepherd, Tessa, and Jessie brings in her two small rescue dogs, Sammy and Coco. Jessie has also taken elders to visit the horses at the property where she keeps her own thoroughbreds.

The other dogs are popular but there was something more that distinguished Ralf, says Jessie. 'Ralf has an aura about him and not every dog has that—they might be cute but they don't have that serene aura. It's like he's been here before.'

The people at Trinity Manor became like a family on the periphery of her own, Caroline says. And losing touch with any of its members—as Alzheimer's closed them down, or as their health gave in to old age—was always hard. Some she could feel slipping away mentally in front of her—there one minute, absent forever the next. Others were gone physically the next time she visited. Most difficult of all for Caroline were the residents her own age who had an acquired brain injury. One woman had a husband the same age as Sam who came in every day to visit her.

But the rewards to Caroline were constant. 'Ralf could move an unhappy moment, hour or three hours really quickly and turn it into a different mood,' she says.

In August 2013, after more than six years, Caroline and Ralf stopped going to Trinity Manor. Rebecca, then eighteen, had become very ill with mumps at a critical time in her education and Caroline wanted to care for her at home. Rebecca had a high temperature for nine weeks.

'Caroline's the most amazing lady,' says Jessie. 'She has the patience of Jove, she understands people with dementia and in aged care. When she sees a person, she doesn't see the illness but the person themselves. She had a better rapport with some people than me! She's just a beautiful, bright personality.'

Jessie says working with people with mental health issues is, by nature, draining, particularly getting close to people who pass away, but Caroline took it all on board and was always positive.

'We view Ralf and Caroline as part of the family,' Jessie says. 'When Ralf came in he brought an element of magic. He helped us see the best in people, helped us see them come out from the shadow of dementia. He really made a difference to peoples' lives.'

Both of them are missed.

16

THE WONDERFUL WORLD OF ANIMAL THERAPY

Caroline took Ralf to a dog clipper near the Victoria Market every six weeks, leading him around with her through the fruit and vegetable stalls at the market afterwards as she shopped. She was often approached on her way through the aisles by people asking about him, and on one occasion was chatting to the parents of a Down's Syndrome child while their son patted Ralf. During the conversation, the child's mother mentioned that The Royal Children's Hospital ran a program using therapy dogs. Ralf would make a good therapy dog, she suggested.

Caroline's interest was piqued. She rang the hospital and was put through to Brenda Kittelty, who managed the visiting volunteers. Caroline explained about Ralf and asked if they could take part in the program. Brenda told her she'd love to have them. First, though, Caroline had to get the necessary paperwork approved and undergo police checks, including the Working With Children check. Ralf would need to be assessed for the program by the Lort Smith Animal Hospital, which oversees the volunteers and their dogs. Caroline had never heard of the animal hospital but took down the details of its volunteer coordinator.

Lort Smith, as it's known, is Australia's biggest not-for-profit animal hospital. It's open every day of the year, employs forty vets and sixty veterinary nurses, treats 40,000 animals a year and has a 15-million-dollar annual budget. It's located not far from The Royal Children's Hospital, in a back street of North Melbourne, in a white, glass-fronted building with a tin roof and an outbuilding that houses offices and administrative staff.

At first glance it could be any other large veterinary institution: lino floors with a bucket and mop handy for accidents, a weighing machine, racks with bags of pet food and shelves with the usual range of pet paraphernalia; bowls, balls, toys, muzzles, harnesses, leads, tags and chewie treats. There's a fully stocked animal pharmacy to one side of the central atrium, a counter manned by staff in royal blue-and-white Lort Smith polo tops, and corridors leading off to treatment rooms.

In the middle of it all, people and their pets wait on rows of plastic seats; dogs on leads, cats in baskets, the occasional bird in a covered cage, and mysterious boxes of various sizes. Owners check out each others' animals, peering into covered cages and baskets, striking up conversations with whomever they're sitting next to. A doctor's surgery is silent; a veterinary waiting room is alive with talk of loved animal companions, their characters and their ailments.

The wonderful world of animal therapy

Look around and you'll see all manner of people and pets. A nervous, chunky-headed Staffy cowering under the seat next to its owner, its incongruously thin tail curled, shaking, between its back legs. A grizzled man in a faded blue flanellette shirt and tracksuit pants cradles a bug-eyed Chihuahua-cross to his chest. An older teenage girl carrying a rucksack holds a blue parrot on her lap, its red beak popping out of the jumper she's wrapped it in. A well-dressed woman with a perfect bob prefers to stand as she waits, her neatly clipped Labradoodle in front of her a model of good behaviour. Every now and then there's a whimper, a mew or a 'Sit!'

But there are also a few signs that Lort Smith's work goes much further than veterinary care.

A brochure on the counter advertises a chaplain, who counsels grief-stricken owners over the death or sickness of a pet, phoning many of those who've just farewelled one and writing to all of them. Bereaved pet owners can grieve for an animal as much as—and sometimes more than—people who have lost a human loved one. Plaques speak of benefactors who care enough about the Lort Smith's work to donate generously.

For the Lort Smith is an organisation with heart.

It provides emergency services. An ambulance waiting in the car park picks up the sick or injured pets of people who don't have transport. It shelters and rehomes domestic animals that have been surrendered or abandoned, and cares for wild ones in an Exotic and Native Wildlife unit, one of its eleven wards. It sends rescue teams to bushfires and other natural disasters to provide emergency on-the-ground veterinary care and support to owners.

Lort Smith also has a social mission.

The organisation runs an Emergency Boarding program with human welfare agencies to care for the pets of people who are elderly or have psychiatric issues, who might have to go into hospital or some form of care such as the Melbourne Clinic, a mental health service. It looks after the pets of homeless people in crisis accommodation and women escaping violent partners.

Liz Walker, CEO and a vet herself, has been at the helm of the Lort Smith Animal Hospital since June 2010. A personable woman who's both compassionate and dynamic, Liz believes pets are a great source of comfort in difficult times.

'Animals are a huge vehicle for happiness,' says Liz, 'especially for people who are marginalised, lonely or have a mental illness—pets don't judge them and have nice values themselves. They're often key to their day-to-day existence—they give them a reason to get up in the morning.'

Liz says there are people enduring enormous hardships to stay with a loved pet; living on the streets if they're not allowed to keep their dog in a rental property or putting up with abuse or a violent relationship for a longer period if it means not having to leave a dog or cat behind. Some people will delay having medical treatment for an illness because they worry about what will happen to their pet. Elderly people fret about their dog or cat being taken away from them if they have to move into aged care.

Lort Smith recognises that the bond between people and their animals can be profound. Take the case of Ham and Pineapple, for example. Ham and Pineapple were rats belonging to a man in his late twenties who was going through a rough patch. The man's marriage had broken down, he'd injured his back, lost his job and had left the family home. But the emergency accommodation he relied on didn't allow animals and after getting caught with his pets a few times he had to give them up. Lort Smith cared for Ham and Pineapple for three months. The man visited them almost every day, sitting on a chair put out for him close to where the rats were housed, reading a book with them on his chest. He eventually put his life back together again and was able to take his pets back to live with him. Liz says, 'Without a doubt those rats helped him connect with the world when everything was going badly and no one cared. They made him feel that life was worth living.'

Liz is also fond of the story of Paul and Roxy. Paul, who was in his sixties and walked with a stick, came to Lort Smith wanting to adopt a Staffordshire Terrier. The staff thought a Staffy might be too vigorous and hard to handle on a lead so introduced Paul to Roxy, a ten-year-old terrier who'd come in for adoption after her owner died. Roxy looked up at Paul with a face that said, 'You need me.' She walked alongside him impeccably, Paul was delighted and the pair left the shelter together. Three days later, Paul had a seizure at home and fell. Roxy, who had been so quiet that her new owner had yet to hear her yap, howled and barked and kept it up until the neighbours came to investigate, peered in the window, saw Paul on the floor and called emergency services. 'Paul just adores Roxy,' says Liz.

The shelter also provides respite care for animals caught in emergencies, such as the time that firefighters rescued an elderly man and his Maltese–Shih Tzu from a house fire. The man was badly burned and was going to be in hospital for a month, leaving his pet with no one to look after it. Lort Smith took the dog in, returning it to its owner once he recovered.

The Lort Smith Animal Hospital was built under the auspices of the Animal Welfare League, which was established in 1927 by, among others, Louisa Lort Smith, a courageous woman passionate about the care of animals. It is run by what is now known as the Animal Welfare League Australia. Originally, the league's main purpose was to help raise money for disadvantaged animals and their owners, with funds divided between the Lost Dogs Home and the Rest Home for Horses, operated by the Victorian Society for the Protection of Animals, the forerunner to the RSPCA (Royal Society for the Prevention of Cruelty to Animals). The Animal Welfare League Hospital opened in Villiers Street, North Melbourne, in 1935, with the aim of reducing the suffering of ill and injured animals while helping their owners. A couple of name changes later and it became the Lort Smith Animal Hospital. The hospital building has also had several metamorphoses since 1935; its current premises were built in 2000.

The organisation now treats pets belonging to owners from all walks of life; from those who go without buying things for themselves to pay for treatment of a treasured pet, to the family that spent $5000 to save a puppy they'd owned for only a few days from a life-threatening illness. It retains its charitable emphasis, giving discounts on veterinary care to people on low incomes and, in dire circumstances, treating a pet without cost. A mother-of-four whose husband had just left her and who had no regular income came to Lort Smith once, distressed, after the family guinea pig broke its leg. The vets who deal with the hospital's small patients—the 'pocket pets'—consulted an orthopaedic surgeon there and jointly devised a pin made of wire to fix the bone in the guinea pig's leg—an operation that otherwise would have been impossibly expensive for the family. It worked—the guinea pig walked again.

Volunteers are still vital to the organisation. More than 500 'vollies', as they're affectionately called, work in the adoption centre cleaning cages or doing whatever's needed, help out in administration, foster kittens or walk dogs. About 150 of them are pet therapy volunteers, fifty-three of whom visit The Royal Children's Hospital.

Lort Smith's pet therapy program visits almost seventy facilities, mostly aged-care institutions, but also hospitals including the oncology ward of the Royal Women's Hospital, psychiatric units, disability services and facilities for people with autism. The program, until recently called PALS (Pets Are Loving Support), was co-founded in 1987 by Joan Ray, working with Guide Dogs Victoria, and was handed over to Lort Smith in 2007. It grew rapidly, especially in recent years, so much so that in 2013 the Lort Smith employed a coordinator solely to handle the therapy dog volunteers. The program is now so popular that there's a waiting list of organisations wanting them.

The demand for therapy dogs has followed widespread and growing awareness of the benefits of animals to health and happiness. The physiological and emotional benefits of the human–animal bond are well documented. Pet owners have been shown to have less physical illness and fewer visits to the doctor; lower incidence of heart attack and stroke; a reduced incidence of childhood allergies; lower rates of depression; and less frequent admission to hospital for those with mental illness. Studies have shown that patting a dog lowers blood pressure, reduces stress and anxiety, and increases calmness and morale. Animals provide a sense of purpose, particularly to those feeling down, and reduce loneliness.

Belief in the healing power of animals dates back to ancient Egypt and Greece when it was often linked to the gods. The idea that dogs could heal injuries, and even cure illnesses, by licking sores and open wounds continued into the Christian era. The use of animals in therapy was first documented by a Quaker, William Tuke, in the late-eighteenth century. Tuke established an asylum in England called the York Retreat, an institution with a humane attitude towards the mentally ill. Rather than being locked up, patients were allowed to wander the grounds of the retreat among domesticated animals. Tuke used farm animals, including rabbits and chickens, as part of his treatment plan, maintaining that it enhanced the 'humanity of the emotionally ill' and helped reduce the use of drugs and restraints. The Bethlem Hospital, also in England—Europe's oldest institution specialising in mental health—followed suit, introducing dogs, cats, birds and goldfish into its wards in 1860.

Sigmund Freud wrote about the psychological value to patients of having a dog in the room. Freud inadvertently observed that his Chow Chow, Jofi, had a calming effect on the children he was psychoanalysing. He noticed, too, that patients, both adults and children, responded more openly to him when she was there and that there was less tension in the room. Freud came to dogs in his latter years, in the mid-1920s, after his daughter Anna bought him an Irish Wolfhound. Jofi, his third dog, became his constant companion, was fed morsels of food from his own plate and sat in on his consultations. She comforted him during the time when he had a series of painful operations for cancer in his jaw.

US psychiatrist Boris Levinson is said to be the first person to have used the term 'pet therapy'. Levinson used his dog Jingles to help him treat children in therapy sessions in the 1960s, after noticing that an otherwise withdrawn nine-year-old boy greeted Jingles enthusiastically when he came into his rooms. The child was wary of talking to Levinson, but he'd happily talk to Jingles. Levinson even called Jingles his 'co-therapist'. In 1961 he presented his findings about the benefits to children of having Jingles in therapy sessions to the American Psychological Association. He later made a number of claims about pets and childhood development, for instance that children exposed to pets could become more sensitive to the feelings of others, more self-accepting and have greater self-control, and that the unconditional affection shown by pets helped them through crises in their lives. He advocated that companion animals could be used, carefully, as a form of therapy in institutions such as nursing homes and hospitals. Levinson's ideas were pooh-poohed by his colleagues at the time—five decades later they're well accepted.

As the positive role of animals in therapy became better understood, the use of trained therapy dogs spread to a broad range of areas. Today, they're used in prisons, hospices, domestic abuse refuges and special education centres, by war veteran groups and in US courtrooms to calm traumatised victims. Other animals that are also enlisted for their therapeutic benefits include: cats (particularly in nursing homes), goldfish (for their calming qualities), dolphins, rabbits, guinea pigs and horses.

For decades, the Riding for the Disabled Association (RDA) in Australia has demonstrated the positive physiological effects of horse riding, which improves muscle tone, muscle strength and coordination in people who may not be able to join in other sports because of a disability. The RDA has shown, too, the joy and sense of confidence that being around a horse brings. Equine Facilitated Learning (EFL), also known as Equine Assisted Therapy, has grown more recently as a treatment in Australia. EFL uses groundwork and horse handling rather than riding, and draws on the communication between horse and human to help improve self-esteem, verbalisation and confidence. It's enlisted for people with autism, bipolar disorder, children with Attention Deficit Disorder, bullies, and victims of bullying, trauma and abuse. In the US, miniature ponies in the not-for-profit charity Therapy Horses of Gentle Carousel visit 25,000 people a year in hospitals, hospices and other centres, and therapeutic ponies are used in Australia, too.

Lort Smith only has dogs in its pet therapy program—but not just any dog. Potential volunteers must complete an application form about their dog's behaviour and the extent of its training, and then have it tested by professional dog handlers and trainers.

By the time they reach the test stage, the applicants have attended an information session explaining the benefits of pet therapy for patients, including accounts of the conditions and illnesses people they might visit might have. They must complete police checks and sign a statutory declaration, and come in for an informal interview.

The assessors decide which environments the dog can handle, whether it be working with children, in aged care, in a psychiatric unit or disability services. Once selected, the volunteers can indicate a preference for an institution they want to visit and attend an induction session to meet its staff, tour the building and to undertake any specific training relevant to that facility. From there on, it's up to the volunteers to make the visits, with Lort Smith's Pet Therapy Program Officer on hand for any queries and to keep check of their progress.

Not many dogs are knocked back, says Sarah DeBorre, the Pet Therapy Program Officer. 'If they're not suitable and don't pass, their owners are given tips afterwards.' The advice might include the owner having a towel on hand if the dog is a slobberer, and training they should be working on if they'd like to reapply (usually in three to six months). Most of the dogs on the program are purebreds, though there are bitsers and rescue dogs too.

Sarah says she often hears stories about how animals can help people. Take Sarah's grandmother for instance. The elderly woman tripped outside her house one frosty Melbourne night and couldn't get back up again. With no one around to help her, she was forced to spend the night outside, in danger of suffering from exposure. Her Labrador-cross lay on top of her all night.

'That dog was usually out-of-control crazy,' says Sarah, 'but it knew something was wrong. My grandmother complained the next day that the dog had squashed her—it was an over-weight Lab—but it saved her.'

Caroline visited the Lort Smith several times, enjoying meeting the enthusiastic band of young women who worked in administration there, but she was keen to get the paperwork through so that she could become accredited. Working with children at The Royal Children's Hospital sounded perfect for Ralf, and she couldn't wait for him to start.

17

MEETING THE KIDS

Brenda Kittelty, who coordinates the visiting volunteer program at The Royal Children's Hospital, recalls vividly the winter's day in 2009 when new recruit Caroline Lovick walked into her office in the Family Resource Centre with Ralf. After several phone conversations, Caroline had come in to finalise her paperwork and be issued with her security pass. She'd told Brenda that she had a Giant Schnauzer; Brenda herself has a Miniature Schnauzer, but had never seen a Giant, so was expecting, perhaps, a larger version of her dog.

'I didn't really have a very solid picture in my mind of what he'd look like,' Brenda says. 'I was gobsmacked when I saw this spectacular animal walk in. He was by far the largest dog we'd had in the hospital, broad across the rump, and those feet!'

The Royal Children's Hospital, in Melbourne's inner-north, is the state's specialist paediatric hospital, handling the gamut of child and adolescent medical problems—everyone from sick or injured children as outpatients, major trauma cases and organ transplant recipients, to adolescents with eating disorders. The Royal Children's also runs health promotion and prevention programs. Its reach includes children from neighbouring states, such as Tasmania and southern New South Wales, as well as those who travel from around Australia and overseas for specialist treatment.

The hospital started bringing in Lort Smith therapy dogs around 2006 when it was in its previous premises—the old hospital as it's called—but only in special circumstances, for instance for a child from a farm who badly missed having an animal around or a recovering trauma patient who was reluctant to participate in physiotherapy. Only dogs that were easy to keep clean, toilet-trained, fully vaccinated, wormed, free of fleas and skin diseases, and with behaviour and temperament assessed by experts were approved. Dogs that jumped on people, barked or were too lively were not allowed.

Susie Knight, then the Adolescents' Ward clerk, was one of the people at the hospital who saw first-hand the benefits of the canine visits, and urged hospital management to introduce a regular program.

Susie had seen dogs used in physiotherapy and occupational and speech therapy. She'd watched as ailing children exclaimed with delight, 'Look, there's a dog coming into my room!' or 'Wait till I tell my friends at school that there are dogs in the hospital!' She'd watched bedridden children overcome their reluctance to move, and children recovering from head injury speak for the first time, at the sight or feel of a dog. She'd witnessed a child seemingly unconscious after surgery open his eyes as his mother said, 'There's a dog here, you've got to see this dog!'

Susie had also seen the positive effects of a dog on staff who were dealing with sometimes sad or stressful situations. She recognised the relief on the faces of parents who were able to talk about something other than their sick child, when a dog visited, and who would often ask for it to be brought in to see their child again.

Word spread throughout the hospital about the canine visits and how well-received they were. The hospital's infection control department felt safer about inviting people in with their dogs as more research and information on infection control became available. Susie was thrilled when the therapy dog visits were formalised in 2008, and has enjoyed watching the program grow and thrive in the years since then.

Caroline and Ralf made their first official visit to the hospital the day after she met Brenda. That morning she parked the car on the outskirts of Royal Park, walking towards the hospital through broad fields edged by eucalypts, Ralf trotting along beside her in his easy, fluid pace. He was jubilant; a new place to walk, new smells, doggie messages left on trees, poles and rubbish bins, other pets and people to meet.

Caroline prepped him on the way: 'Remember, you'll be working. You're going to be really good today. You'll have to really behave yourself, Ralfie.'

But Ralf completely ignored her, she says; the pep talk, she had to admit, was for herself. Caroline was feeling somewhat anxious about the day ahead. 'I wasn't sure that I could do it. I'm a mother of four. I've done a bit in life, I'm out there, but I knew it would be confronting.' She'd never known what would happen on any one day at Trinity Manor, and being at the children's hospital could be even more unpredictable and challenging emotionally.

As they walked through Royal Park, they came across other dogs and their owners who would stop to ask about Ralf and chat with Caroline; though one woman with a little white dog that looked like a slipper steered a wide berth, giving Caroline a look that said, 'Your dog is going to eat my dog'. But there were other dogs for Ralf to meet and greet. A young woman with a Border Collie paused and exclaimed, 'He's a big bear! He's gorgeous! What is he?' The women chatted for a minute while the two dogs sniffed each other and touched noses.

When they were near the hospital—a cream brick slab of a building with multiple rows of small windows—Caroline stopped to remove Ralf's chain and replace it with his red collar. Now he really was in work mode.

It wasn't long before they encountered their first child, a little girl in a wheelchair with her mother on the path ahead. Caroline and Ralf paused as they drew close then stopped as the mother made a cheery remark about Ralf. After Caroline introduced herself to the girl and her mother, Ralf edged up to the chair. He looked the girl in the eyes but turned his head slightly away so she wouldn't feel threatened, and waited. Caroline pulled the wheelchair closer and Ralf lowered his head gently into the girl's lap. A look of delight spread across the girl's face. At that moment, any concerns that Caroline might have had about the day ahead melted away.

As they walked through the hospital's corridors on their way to check in to Brenda's office, Caroline and Ralf met more curious children and adults. Everywhere they went, people stared, smiled, said hello and asked questions. Caroline stopped to talk with anyone who wanted to pat Ralf, answering their inevitable questions of 'What's his name?', 'What breed is he?' and 'How much does he weigh?'

The occasional young child turned to bury their head in their mother's legs and Caroline would smile and quietly keep walking, others clapped their hands with glee at the sight of Ralf and some didn't stop smiling. There were a few adults who looked like they'd had a horrendous day and wanted to hug Ralf too; Ralf obliged as Caroline talked to them. Doctors, nurses and other staff were keen to welcome her, too. A visiting professor from overseas who'd never seen a dog in the ward before paused, amazed, to ask Caroline about their work. A young man just wanted to take a photo for his girlfriend.

'I'm so sorry I'm late,' Caroline apologised as she finally arrived at Brenda's office. 'I've taken a while getting here.'

'Yes, I know,' said Brenda. 'We saw you come into the hospital an hour ago!'

Brenda explained to Caroline about the areas in the hospital where she could and could not go, and spoke about respecting the privacy of families and personal space. From then on, Caroline was always aware that asking to come into someone's hospital room was like asking to enter their bedroom.

That first day was a blur.

To Caroline, the hospital seemed like a rabbit warren of corridors and stairs. Side-tracked by people who'd stop to talk or marvel at Ralf, she became disoriented on several occasions, confused about where they'd been and not been.

The Royal Children's Hospital, before it was rebuilt in 2011, was a tired affair: grey lino floors that were polished and clean but cracked and worn; cold bleak staircases with old metal railings; lifts that were small, slow to arrive and always crowded; and waiting areas that consisted of chairs in hallways a distance from the reception desk to the wards and with no magazines to read. The Family Resource Centre—large, bright and decorated with children's paint-ings—was the exception.

Caroline and Ralf were only allowed in Four North, the orthopaedic ward. Dogs weren't permitted in areas such as intensive care, surgical, cardiac or cancer wards, and were only allowed in on Fridays. Four North was accessed by double doors off a corridor and contained four beds to a room, sepa-rated by curtains on overhead rails. If the curtain was pulled around, it meant the patient required privacy, for instance when they were sleeping, having their dressings changed or undergoing some form of treatment. Caroline would make her presence known and, if asked, would promise to come back. On the other side of a corridor were single rooms with very sick children in them. The bathrooms were communal.

As Caroline entered the rooms she would quickly try to gauge a situation to see whether it was the right time for a visit, then sing out to the parents or family, 'Hi guys, this is Ralfie. He's a therapy dog—would you like a visit?' Ralf would then automatically head towards the young patient. Some children were tentative at first; others immediately squealed with excitement and fussed over Ralf. Caroline felt 'invisible' at his side, as she'd done at Trinity Manor, as all attention turned to him.

Ralf, too, seemed to be able to read a situation. When he saw his first very small child outside a room, he approached her carefully, looked away, then slid slowly down along the floor with his front legs, then his haunches, until he was in a 'drop' position, pressing his nose against the floor—making himself seem as small as possible, every movement passive and controlled.

Occasionally, a child or their parents would decline a visit because they didn't like dogs, were frightened by them or didn't want to be interrupted, and one or two parents in the corridor looked at Ralf askance, not sure what to make of him.

Caroline also met Susie Knight that first day when checking into the adolescent ward.

'Wow, is that a dog?' said Susie cheerfully.

The two women formed an instant rapport—over Ralf, as often happens—and Caroline came to think of the engaging woman with the ear piercings and alternative air about her as her 'eclectic goddess'. Thereafter she would always check in for a chat with Susie first whenever they visited the ward, and as she left she'd be told, 'And don't miss anybody!' If Ralf missed a room in the adolescent ward, there could be an angry or disappointed teen—and Susie Knight to answer to.

She was struck by how enthusiastic the people working at the hospital were, as if they were making up for their drab surrounds, but sensed that some of the parents were dissatisfied—the rooms were cramped ('cupboards', says Caroline) and parents who wanted to stay overnight only had fold-up beds.

At the end of the day, Caroline reported back to Brenda Kittelty. 'This is amazing!' she said. Some cases she'd seen *were* confronting and some were sad but all of it had been rewarding, and Ralf seemed to thrive on meeting the patients.

After that first day, Caroline left the hospital exhausted and elated. Ralf became a 'normal' dog again, trotting in the park, head high, scanning the grasslands for some action, until he got back into the car where he stretched the length of the back seat, put his head between his front paws, sighed deeply and fell asleep.

That day set the pattern for hundreds of visits that followed. Ralf and Caroline visited The Royal Children's Hospital every second Friday, and Trinity Manor every second Wednesday. The walk through Royal Park to the hospital became longer: Ralf liked to stop and greet people on the way, taking his time and heading towards every child he saw, Caroline following. It was important that he did, she says; they might see a patient who was new to the hospital and needed some encouragement to be there, or an 'old friend' who might be feeling fragile and would be upset if Ralf passed by them. What should be a five-minute walk usually took twenty-five minutes.

Their hospital rounds developed a warm familiarity. Caroline would always preface a visit to young children with, 'Do you want a play date?' To tentative children, she'd say, 'Maybe you'd just like to wave at Ralfie?' Or else she'd give them a confidential look and say, 'He's really a horse,' which somehow made Ralf less of a giant dog. She'd joke to brown-eyed children they must be twins with Ralf, and she would tell children who were in for a long stay that the hospital 'only keeps the good ones'.

Caroline never asked relatives the reason for their child's stay in hospital, or talked about how awful an accident or illness it must have been—that was the last topic anxious parents wanted to discuss. But she picked up on levels of sickness and levels of sadness. Sometimes she sensed an 'elephant in the room'.

'You don't know whether the child's been fighting to get back from something and isn't going to make it,' she says. 'It's the conversation you never have.'

She talked instead about anything and everything else, drawing from her own life, from things she and her family had done together. She'd tell them about the time Ed broke his leg and the way Ralf sat on his bed next to him while he was recovering. If the child's family were from the country, she'd talk about their horses or recent floods or recall an occasion when the Lovick children competed in a sporting event up their way. Caroline, who grew up in country UK, liked talking to people from the land, to 'parents who get excited by the mention of tractors and loaders'. She remembered tidbits about families of children she saw regularly so she could ask them questions from visit to visit.

Caroline made sure she was always upbeat on her rounds, doling out what she calls her 'bit of happy' on the way. 'It's TLC help yourself day!' she'd say to anyone who looked upset.

She sensed the trauma some parents were experiencing. She had once sat in a chair at The Royal Children's Hospital desperately hoping that a nurse or doctor would come over to her and say, 'Your child's well—you can go home now'.

It was 10 November 2007, the night of the party for Ed's eleventh birthday. Imogen, then sixteen years old, said she felt unwell and would stay home while the family went out. Caroline came home to find her curled up in bed, groggy and not making any sense. She felt her daughter's brow. 'You could have fried an egg on it.'

Caroline immediately drove Imogen to The Royal Children's Emergency department where she was rushed through the waiting area to a consulting room. What seemed like twenty doctors flooded into the room, discussing symptoms then each departing as their area of expertise was ruled out. The doctors suspected meningitis—inflammation of the brain and spinal cord—which can be fatal. There was talk of a lumbar puncture, hurried discussions about what else might be wrong with Imogen. Caroline was absolutely terrified. 'It was like watching a wave crash over you.'

After four days of visits to the hospital Imogen was finally diagnosed with thyroiditis, which was then treated with antibiotics. The experience gave Caroline a glimpse into what it must be like for the parents with a child at the hospital. 'I felt like hell. And that was only for four days—not the four months that some parents wait for their child to have a transplant.

I think now, "I'll do anything to make your child smile, to make you smile, to make your life a bit better.'"

Caroline became more used to handling the sad or difficult situations she encountered on her rounds, maintaining her 'happy mask' as she met children who she suspected were not going home or who looked sad alongside their anxious parents. 'You get better at it. You can't react.'

Occasionally, though, it all got too much for her and the mother-of-four would head down to Brenda Kittelty's office and cry.

'You have to be kinder to yourself, take more care of yourself,' Brenda would advise her.

She was used to counselling volunteers, debriefing them after something they'd seen and heard. 'Visiting can be tough,' she says. 'There are a lot of happy stories that come out of here but there are some really sad ones. That's life on the wards. It's not all about kids getting well, unfortunately, and some families deal with that better than others.'

Brenda adds, 'It can be a bit confronting but Caroline's got a lot of resilience and life experience—and she's the mother of four older children herself.'

As for Ralf, the only time he looked uneasy was when they visited a child with a tracheostomy and tubes pumping air to their lungs—confused, he would look either side of the device to find out where the breathing was coming from.

Ralf quickly became popular at the hospital. So much so that parents began asking for their appointments to be on Friday, so they could tell their children that they were going to the hospital 'to see Ralf'.

'For kids who are going in to have unpleasant procedures or needles stuck in them, if their parents can sell the idea that "We're going to visit Ralf" it makes all the difference,' says Caroline.

Doctors on wards where Ralf wasn't allowed to visit asked if they could perhaps bring little Ella or Andrew to him instead, and would meet in one of Ralf's wards. If a child was due to have an operation or a procedure that they were anxious about, Ralf would be called in by the staff to act as a diversion. He was sometimes co-opted to accompany a frightened child being wheeled to theatre or to encourage a child to behave. Nurses asked Caroline if Ralf could sit with small children who were having their blood taken to distract them from the needle going into their arm.

Susie also enlisted Ralf for problem patients in her ward. Once she called Caroline to help with a teenager who had become well enough to walk but whose recovery had stalled because he didn't want to get out of bed and do physiotherapy. 'Has a bit of attitude,' Susie said. Caroline didn't know what was wrong with the boy and didn't ask. She *did* know that Susie only called if she really needed her help.

They brought Ralf in and after introductions, the physiotherapist asked, 'Would you like to take the dog for a walk?'

'Can I, really?' the boy said, instantly perking up.

With help from the physiotherapist and Susie, the teenager was soon walking, in stiff, slow motions, with Ralf and Caroline in the corridor. Caroline recalls that the lanky youth didn't respond to her at all, cutting her short whenever she spoke, and focused all his attention on Ralf as if the dog was the only one who understood him.

For a few weeks after that, Caroline and Ralf alternated with another volunteer and dog on a roster of two consecutive days each, trying to keep the teenager on his feet. 'You're in the fight with them and giving them the tools,' Caroline explains. She doesn't know what happened to the boy—only that he was bedridden when she first visited and he was walking again when she last saw him. 'If you can get a child to be active again, life starts to take over and they do it themselves,' she says.

Susie recalls a girl who'd had a stroke and couldn't use one side of her body reaching out unexpectedly to Ralf one day. Her father, standing by her bed, gasped. 'She put out her stroke arm!' he said. Susie got goosebumps, as she sometimes does when she's watching Ralf with the patients. 'I just wanted to cry,' she says, 'but I can't—I'm staff here!'

Caroline later increased her visits to one day a week—and sometimes more often—and became one of the hospital's most frequent dog therapy volunteers. 'That team together is amazing,' Susie says. 'Caroline never knocks back a request for an extra visit, and she'll come in during her holidays if Ralf's needed.' Susie will often see Caroline in the morning then again three hours later: 'Are you still here!'

She says that Ralf became one of the dogs that parents and children asked for most often. 'He's a very special boy. It's not just his size, it's his nature. People remember "the black pug" or "the beige labrador" but everyone remembers Ralf by name.'

18

NEW GROUND

In October 2011 the old Royal Children's Hospital was replaced by much larger premises built on a site next to it. It began a new era for the institution and for all the lives it touched—patients, parents, staff and visitors, including Caroline and Ralf.

The hospital was originally called Melbourne's Free Hospital for Sick Children. Its first incarnation was a terrace building in the CBD before it moved to another terrace in Pelham Street, Carlton, in 1876. Just as she had officially opened the hospital's Flemington Road site in 1963, the Queen opened the latest building on 26 October 2011. The new hospital cost one billion dollars and took four years to construct. Almost a month later, on 20 November, the patients in the old hospital were transferred in a military-style operation to the new one through a tunnel built between the two buildings.

An orientation day was held for staff and the volunteers asked to attend, without their dogs. Caroline entered the hospital and immediately thought it was stunning. 'Main Street', as the airy central atrium is called, is six storeys high and stretches from Flemington Road to Royal Park. It's overhung by a two-storey-tall sculpture, a squiggly harlequin-like creature with a butterfly on its tongue. Caroline joined the other therapy dog owners assembling at the white loop-shaped reception desk she calls 'the potty'—the first time she'd met up with them in the hospital as a group. She recognised a few faces from Lort Smith functions and had heard about other volunteers through patients, their parents or staff. Caroline was surprised by the number of people who approached her and said, 'Oh, so *you're* Ralf's mum!'

They were shown to a theatrette for a briefing about the new hospital, Caroline scanning the rows as she took her seat, spotting faces of staff she knew. The group was then taken on a tour. As ambassadors for the hospital, they needed to know where everything was, including the areas that were off-limits to dogs. Caroline says it's useful to know practical information such as where hospital visitors can recharge their phones or directions to the Victoria Market, questions she is sometimes asked.

There were visual delights at every turn. Animal and nature murals on the walls, a two-storey-high reef aquarium with tropical fish and small sharks in the Emergency waiting room, a sky garden. There's a meerkat colony near the outpatients area and landscaped courtyards for children to play in. There's even a cinema with bean bags. Throughout the new building, windows open to views of the surrounding parklands, and the rooms are full of colour—bright mobiles, cheerful bedspreads, funky orange and green light fittings.

'The staff were thrilled to bits with the new hospital,' Caroline says. 'Everyone was really proud. Every fundraising event, every knitted hat and every stuffed toy they'd sold, everything the hospital auxiliary had done had been working towards this.'

She couldn't wait to come back with Ralf.

Their first day, however, didn't begin well. When Caroline arrived with Ralf, five security guards sighted them and stormed towards her. 'What are you doing bringing that dog into the hospital?' one demanded to know. The men soon began to look sheepish as Caroline explained that Ralf, wearing his new security pass, was part of the therapy dog team. 'Okay then,' they said, changing their tune and backing off. 'Nice dog!'

Towards the end of the time at the old hospital, Brenda Kittelty received more and more requests from doctors and staff asking if dogs could visit their wards, too. The shift to the new building had brought with it changes in work practices, a chance for hospital management and staff to think about the ways the hospital operated and what could be done differently—including a greater role for therapy dogs. With the new premises, the number of wards that accommodated dog therapy grew, as did the numbers of volunteers. Ralf now had four wards to visit instead of just two.

New ground

The new wards were arranged in pods—rooms in a loop around a central administrative area with a sleek, curvy desk. The single rooms with their ensuites looked to Caroline like motel rooms. There were also double rooms for siblings, placed together to help reduce the trauma of being away from home and in a strange environment. Caroline and Ralf began a new routine, working their way around the rooms of each ward in each loop, starting from the left, Caroline memorising the ones they'd missed and would have to return to, never forgetting Susie Knight's warning not to miss anyone.

Ralf's back leg shook at the sight of the new rooms in the wards with their vinyl divans. 'Every room had a spare "dog bed"—the children's parents thought it was for them to sleep on but Ralf knew it was for him!' says Caroline. He was, of course, allowed on the lounges and beds at home. The patients' beds were lower and simpler to move up and down, which made it easier for Ralf to climb on. He always made himself comfortable when he was on a bed, watching cartoons with the child if they featured animals or lying alongside them as they fell asleep.

After finishing the rooms in the wards, Caroline and Ralf visited the outpatients and specialists' area on the ground floor, where parents and children waited to be called into consulting and treatment rooms. Some were coming into the hospital for the first time, others with familiar faces were back for follow-up appointments. The area was busy, with families milling around between the central lounge seats and the child-sized plastic tables and chairs. It faces onto the meerkat enclosure, a courtyard enclosed by floor-to-ceiling glass.

The meerkat colony was an attraction from the start—parents and patients were mesmerised at the sight of the expressive little beady-eyed creatures running up and down logs and rocks and onto the ground near the windows. There is always one meerkat standing high on the rocks on its hind legs, body propped up by its tail, swivelling its head this way then that on the lookout for danger, protecting the colony as it would in the wilds of southern Africa. They've adapted well to hospital life, though early on the meerkats mistook the hospital's emergency helicopter for a giant predator, perhaps a hawk or eagle, when it flew over them, which upset them. Ralf was interested but he'd seen meerkats before on TV so settled down and watched them, relaxed, as he would do at home, while the children came to sit around him on the floor. Curiously, the meerkats didn't seem at all perturbed by Ralf, approaching the glass to have a closer look at him.

Caroline and Ralf's final visit on their first day at the new hospital was to the Emergency department where, amid the drama and dismay of sudden illness and broken limbs, they took time out to look at the aquarium. Ralf had seen fish before—having watched *Finding Nemo* and taken a close interest in the Lovicks' goldfish in the ponds at home—and he found the enormous aquarium fascinating.

They left nearly four hours after they'd arrived, having covered more ground than they'd ever done before and discovering new aspects of the hospital they'd have to learn about. Caroline says, 'It was almost like starting over again—a new adventure for Ralf and me.'

19

ZEKE, THE BOY WHO LAUNCHED THE DOG

In late 2010 Jazmin Hall was living a quiet life in country Victoria, sharing a home with her truck-driver husband Corey Harrison and their three-year-old son Jacob in the wheat town of Wycheproof, in the state's north-west. Wycheproof is a typical Aussie country town—it has a grand red-brick pub called the Royal Mail, and a smaller one called the Terminus, verandahed shops, a historic courthouse, silos on the rail line and a racetrack. The town has a proud sporting history, producing a number of AFL players, and two other claims to fame: a functioning railway line that runs along a median strip in the main street, and the world's smallest registered mountain. Mount Wycheproof 'soars'—as the local tourism authority good humouredly puts it—at 43 metres above sea level, in an otherwise flat landscape. Like many other country towns, Wycheproof has struggled to maintain its population, which numbers in the mere hundreds, even offering houses for rent at a dollar a week in 2009, in a bid to lure people to live there. Jazmin Hall would be one of the people joining the exodus.

She was nine months pregnant with their second baby in December 2010 when floodwaters surrounded the town. It had been a straightforward pregnancy but she was overdue, as she'd been with first child Jacob. Her doctor thought it best to admit her to Bendigo Health's hospital, 135 kilometres away, in case she went into labour and was unable to leave Wycheproof and reach the hospital in time. As with Jacob's birth it was to be a natural delivery with no drugs. Jazmin, then aged twenty-two, knew that the baby was going to be quite big but she was expecting it to be another uncomplicated delivery. The sex of the child, though, was going to be a surprise.

Jazmin was induced ten days after she went into hospital and Zeke was born on 7 December; Corey and Jazmin's grandmother at her side, a midwife and nurse helping her to deliver. But as the baby's crown appeared, the midwife told Jazmin the umbilical cord was wrapped around its neck. They worked swiftly to free the cord.

Jazmin waited to hear its first cry. Seconds passed.

'Is my baby okay?' she asked. 'What's wrong? Why is the baby not crying? Is it a girl or boy?'

With little warning, the nurse activated a Code Blue alert—within minutes the room was filled with doctors and nurses. Corey and her grandmother quickly stepped to one side. The baby was taken to another part of the room. As the doctors and nurses busied themselves around the infant, Jazmin sat in bed, helpless to act and listening for a cry. She ached to hold her baby.

'Just try to keep calm,' one of the nurses said. 'We're just trying to help your baby to breathe. It'll be fine.'

Corey, too, tried to reassure his wife, although he, like Jazmin, didn't know what was happening. A few minutes later one of the nurses came over to her and announced, 'Congratulations on a beautiful baby boy.'

But there was still no sound from him.

From the time Zeke was born it took eight excruciating minutes for him to cry. Jazmin and Corey heard him yell, and heaved a collective sigh of relief. She had been administered Pethidine an hour before the birth, which had depressed his respiration; Zeke had been administered a narcotic antagonist during resuscitation to get him breathing properly. One of the nurses brought him to her to hold, briefly, before he was taken away to the Special Care Baby Unit.

As Corey looked after Jacob, mother and son spent another night in hospital, before Jazmin could take Zeke home. He was feeding properly and was an apparently healthy baby.

Zeke slept and fed well during his stay in hospital, drinking a combination of breast and formula milk, but when he arrived home he stopped feeding, refusing to take milk or spitting it out. He was sleeping for what seemed like abnormally long periods of time and when he awoke, he'd scream as if in pain. He hardly wee'd and didn't open his bowels.

Jazmin called the phone service Nurse on Call, for advice about Zeke's behaviour. She took him to a local doctor's surgery. She worried aloud too to the domiciliary nurse about him. They all assured her that Zeke had had a traumatic birth and would soon come good.

'I said to the nurse, "There's definitely something wrong with him—he's hardly drunk anything." I told her that Zeke still hadn't opened his bowels after six days.' Still, Jazmin was told he'd be okay.

The next day, she was considering taking her son back to the hospital at Bendigo when she answered the phone to a voice she didn't recognise.

The woman introduced herself as being a metabolic specialist from The Royal Children's Hospital, and asked her, 'Do you have a baby called Zeke Harrison?'

Jazmin confirmed she did.

'How is he?'

'Actually, he's not well,' said Jazmin and started to describe Zeke's behaviour to the woman.

'There are some problems with his bloods—his newborn screening test,' the specialist said. 'We've sent an ambulance to your house. You need to put your child in it. This is crucial.'

Before Jazmin had a chance to ask any questions, the woman continued, 'I'll call you back soon—I need to confirm with the other doctors what's happening,' and ended the call.

Jazmin was reeling as she ran from room to room, trying to pack a bag with things she'd need for Zeke, so nervous and perplexed she couldn't think of what to pack.

The specialist rang back soon afterwards, explaining that the lab results of Zeke's heel-prick test—the test all three-day-old babies have to detect disease and disorders—showed that he had Maple Syrup Urinary Disease (MSUD), a rare and life-threatening condition that affects the way the body tolerates protein. The formula milk Zeke was having, as well as the first few days of breast milk, had turned into toxins in his body. His body's way of countering the toxins was to stop feeding. 'He's a very sick baby—he needs urgent medical attention,' the specialist said. 'We have to act quickly.'

Jazmin immediately phoned Corey, still confused by the news she'd been given. He was on the road driving a truck at the time and said he'd join her in Melbourne after he'd returned from the trip. In the meantime Corey's father would look after Jacob.

An hour later, an ambulance driver knocked on Jazmin's door and helped her into the back of the vehicle with Zeke, instructing her on the way to hold an oxygen mask over her son's face and check the oxygen and blood pressure monitors—there was no second paramedic. Jazmin was by now terrified.

As they drove off, she clutched her week-old baby to her chest, watching the oxygen levels on the monitor rise and fall and calling out statistics to the paramedic every few minutes. The ambulance officer headed for Wycheproof hospital but was informed during the trip that the hospital didn't have the equipment required to treat Zeke and that he would have to keep driving. The paramedic stopped the ambulance briefly at the station in Charlton, the next town, to pick up a baby capsule, relieving Jazmin of holding Zeke. The metabolic team at The Royal Children's Hospital instructed the paramedic to take Zeke to Bendigo hospital where their neonatal emergency transport team would meet Jazmin and Zeke to transfer him from there to The Royal Children's.

Zeke was taken from Jazmin as soon as they arrived at the emergency department at Bendigo. What seemed like a surfeit of curious doctors filed into the room keen to familiarise themselves with the unusual disease, and were soon handing around a vial of Zeke's urine, and sniffing it. 'It was so odd,' says Jazmin.

One of the doctors explained to her that the sample smelt like maple syrup, hence the name of the condition. At the time Jazmin had noticed that the little urine Zeke had passed at home smelt unusual but hadn't thought much of it. The disease was so rare that only one doctor at Bendigo, who'd just returned from overseas, knew about it. 'Everyone else was looking it up on the computer,' says Jazmin.

Soon the doctors were pushing a nasal gastric tube through Zeke's nose to his stomach to deliver a special formula to counteract the toxins accumulating in his body, and were pricking him many times over with a needle to take more samples of blood. By now it was almost midnight and Corey had returned home from work. Jazmin updated her husband on what was happening, and, concerned for his safety, suggested he sleep for a few hours before driving the three hours to Melbourne. Corey tossed and turned as he tried to rest, not knowing if Zeke was going to survive the night.

A few hours later the three-person neonatal team arrived from Melbourne and put mother and child in the back of the ambulance with a nurse. Zeke fell in and out of consciousness during the journey, resuscitated four times after his breathing stopped.

They arrived at The Royal Children's Hospital at 2.30 a.m. where the unconscious baby was taken to neonatal ICU. The metabolic team talked to Jazmin to explain further the risks to Zeke's health, their diagnosis and Zeke's treatment. Jazmin learned that even tiny amounts of proteins could result in Zeke's brain swelling and cause seizures. Her world was becoming more fraught by the minute. The doctors explained that Zeke might need to be put on haemfiltration—dialysis to filter out the toxins in his blood—and advised Jazmin to get some sleep in the emergency accommodation room nearby until they knew if, and when, this would be done. It was now 4.30 a.m. Jazmin resisted leaving, but the doctors insisted that she get some rest. 'We'll call you if anything happens,' they promised.

Jazmin lay curled up on the bed. She flicked the light off and tried to sleep, but her mind kept ticking over. 'Every emotion going through me,' she recalls. Her phone rang half an hour later.

'You need to come back right now,' said the doctor. 'We're putting your son on dialysis—his body is shutting down. If we don't get him on dialysis now, he could die.'

Jazmin waited in the corridor outside the emergency room as doctors performed the operation that would allow them to connect Zeke to the dialysis machine. She walked up and down the corridor. She stared at the door, waiting for news. Looked at the floor, paced some more. As she did, Corey, distressed, made arrangements for the trip to Melbourne. He phoned his father asking him to mind Jacob, then his boss, trying to explain what was happening but failing to get out anything other than, 'He's on life support.' Jazmin was eventually allowed in to see her baby. She was shocked by his appearance: still, puffy and bloodied. One machine was circulating blood, a ventilator was helping him breathe artificially, there were two tubes through his nose and tubes in his pelvis.

And so Jazmin began her vigil in ICU. Sleep was impossible, nor had she eaten anything since the previous day. All she could do was sit and watch, feeling alone and helpless as her son fought for his life. Later in the morning her stepmother Annette and a friend Tamara arrived to offer words of support and welcome hugs. Then, finally, Corey arrived at eleven. Jazmin offered to show him a photo of Zeke on her phone to prepare him for what he was about to see. 'But I just wanted to see my little boy,' he says. Corey sobbed at the sight of his son. 'It was a massive shock to see your baby one day who seemed to be okay, to seeing him all wired up and not responsive to the next.' They all sat together watching over Zeke.

20

ZEKE MEETS RALF

It took four days for the dialysis to clear Zeke's body of toxins. On the sixth day in ICU Jazmin and Corey watched as a light turned green on the ventilator—Zeke had started to breathe on his own. He was slowly improving. It was lucky he was a big baby, she thought, or he'd have faded away by now.

On 17 December they saw their baby boy's eyes again. The doctor slowly reduced Zeke's morphine and sedatives and the baby tried to awaken. A day at a time, Jazmin said to herself. Zeke moved his head and arms not long after that. He was then taken off the ventilator and began to open his eyes for a minute or two at a time. Every small sign of progress was a source of amazement to his mother. On the seventh day in hospital Jazmin was overwhelmed when she was finally allowed to hold him.

Despite the angst, she says she always knew Zeke would recover. Call it a mother's instinct. 'He'd started life as a fighter.'

But her troubles had barely begun.

After ten days in ICU, Zeke was moved to the neurological ward where his brain could be monitored. On 21 December he was transferred back to Bendigo Health's hospital and spent Christmas there with his family. As Jazmin nursed her son, Corey returned to Wycheproof to continue working the three jobs needed for the family to survive and to pay for Zeke's medical bills. They were reunited as a family in Wycheproof just before New Year's Day.

Zeke recovered well but life was difficult for the family once he was home.

A nurse had to be on hand to insert the nasal gastric tube, which was removed once Zeke was feeding well. Then Jazmin had to learn how to do it herself. The first time she had to push the tube through his nose was nerve-racking and she felt for him every time she had to do it. Much later, when Zeke learned to talk, he would plead with her, 'No, Mummy, no.' She and Corey also took blood samples.

The doctors told them that Zeke's MSUD would have to be managed for the rest of his life. He would have special formula every day and blood tests each week. His diet would be strict: no meat, no dairy and a limited quantity of fruit and vegetables. In years to come, every effort would have to be made to prevent other people—his brothers, relatives, kindergarten teachers and school mates—from giving him the wrong foods. He could never play football or other high-impact sports because a broken arm, torn calf muscle or nosebleed would instantly release protein into his blood. He was so often lethargic, Jazmin wondered if Zeke would have the energy to ever play sport anyway.

Jazmin and Corey learned as much as they could about MSUD, finding out that it affects one in 185,000 children and is caused when both parents carry the MSUD gene. By pure bad luck, Jazmin and Corey both carried the gene, giving their offspring a one-in-four chance of inheriting the disease. The couple checked but there had been no history of MSUD on either side of the family.

The slightest contact with a cold or virus would send Zeke back to hospital. He was hospitalised twenty-eight times before his first birthday. For the first three years of his life, he would average an admission a month, staying from three days to two months, accompanied by his parents. Says Jazmin, 'I did everything I could to make him feel comfortable. I'd lie in the cot with him or hold him whenever I could to keep him calm.'

Jazmin and Corey separated when Zeke was eight months old. She left Wycheproof for Melbourne to be nearer The Royal Children's Hospital, staying with family and friends until she found a house of her own on the city's northern fringes. Living with a child with MSUD was exhausting: constant care, long days, sometimes sleepless nights and missed social outings. Keeping Jacob entertained while she cared for Zeke was often difficult too. The day after giving birth to her third son, Sebastian (who has a different father), Jazmin discharged herself from hospital so that she could tend to Zeke, who was sick at home. There were days she felt like she was going to have a breakdown. The fortnightly 1200-kilometre return trips Corey made to relieve Jazmin of the pressures of caring for Zeke also took their toll on him. But, 'I was rewarded seeing my son's eyes light up whenever I arrived at the ward.'

Zeke met Ralf in March 2012 when he was fifteen months old and in The Royal Children's Hospital with a virus. He was unwell and grizzly, and after ten days in isolation he was bored at being confined. 'He didn't want a bar of anything,' says Jazmin. 'He was even bored with his toys.'

Ralf walked into the room and Zeke instantly perked up, standing up by the bars of his cot, pointing at Ralf, his little legs stomping up and down. Caroline introduced herself and Ralf, and was told how frustrated the toddler was at being bedridden.

'Do you want to take Ralfie for a walk?' Caroline asked. Jazmin lifted the excited boy out, as surprised and pleased as he was at the arrival of the furry visitor. Zeke had just learned to walk and set off tottering out of his room, clasping a handful of Ralf's fur. He toddled down the corridor and back with Ralf, then lay with his head on Ralf's stomach.

'It just made him so much happier,' says Jazmin. 'My stepmother has a dog so he loves them. I was happy just to see his little smile. And Ralf's adorable.'

It was a brief encounter but one that would soon be noticed around the world.

The Good Friday Appeal was on so the *Herald Sun* newspaper, wanting to do a story about Ralf the 'dog doctor' at the time, photographed him with Zeke, who was wearing his legless jumpsuit and nappies, and still had a gastric nasal tube. The story, which also featured an account of the way Ralf helped two-year-old Claire Couwenberg walk again after surgery, appeared on 20 March.

Zeke's photo went viral, spreading everywhere as the world's media picked up the story. Jazmin was stunned when someone from the hospital told her it had been published in the *Daily Mail* in the UK.

Soon after, Zeke appeared in other stories about his stays at The Royal Children's Hospital. One featured the hospital's Good Friday Appeal in 2012. Jazmin and Corey had always wanted to give back to the hospital that had saved their son's life. Corey and his new partner Laura Bish organised a fund-raiser in Wycheproof with all proceeds donated to the appeal. Jazmin attended the event with family, missing a fundraiser the following year due to Zeke's health. More than $35,000 was donated in those two years. 'Team Zeke', as they call them-selves, set up a website and plan to run the event annually.

Zeke had his first seizure when he was ten months old. To Jazmin, it seemed as if he was daydreaming. She couldn't get his attention—it was as if he couldn't see her. The 'absent seizures' usually lasted only seconds, at most three minutes, and were relatively harmless. But then, at two and a half years of age, Zeke had what's called a tonic-clonic or grand mal seizure.

Zeke was in hospital at the time, sitting on Jazmin's lap watching television. She noticed his legs become stiff, then his hands clamp before his whole body began spasming.

Immediately she knew what was happening but that didn't lessen her fright as the little boy convulsed in her arms. The nurses, hearing her call out, came to her aid. Zeke's airways were closing. They swiftly took him from Jazmin and laid him down, holding his head up to clear his airways.

Zeke was to have several tonic-clonic seizures after that one, all at home. He would be reserved and depressed for two weeks after each seizure and his speech—and any other skills he was learning at the time—would regress.

Jazmin wasn't aware that there was a cure for MSUD when she was first told about the condition but she researched the disease on the internet and joined several Facebook support groups. In the course of this she met an American woman called Teddi online. Teddi's son had once had MSUD and she told Jazmin that her boy had been freed of the disease after receiving a liver transplant. Interested, Jazmin approached the metabolic team at The Royal Children's Hospital about the possibility. She was told that they wouldn't usually ask the transplant team about a new liver for a patient with MSUD unless it was a particularly serious case because a liver transplant is a very high-risk operation. Jazmin insisted that Zeke's case *was* serious.

The teams conferred, decided that Zeke was a suitable candidate and accepted him for transplant assessment. They warned Jazmin that there was a 15 per cent risk that he could die during the surgery. Jazmin and Corey discussed with the transplant teams what would be involved and agreed to sign

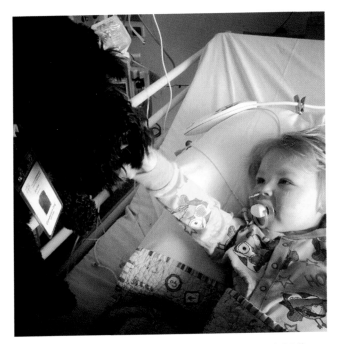

Zeke Harrison with Ralf in The Royal Children's Hospital, Melbourne.

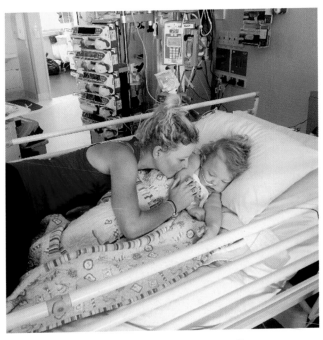

Zeke with his mother, Jazmin Hall.

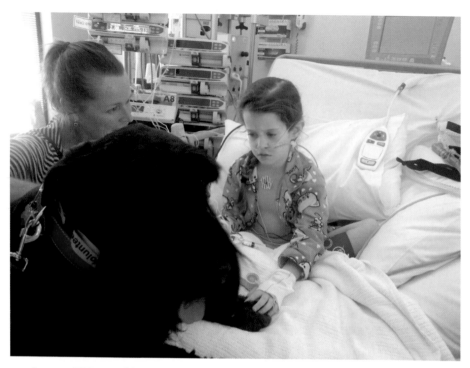

Summer Wilson and her mother Samantha Brew meet Ralf in the Intensive Care Unit.

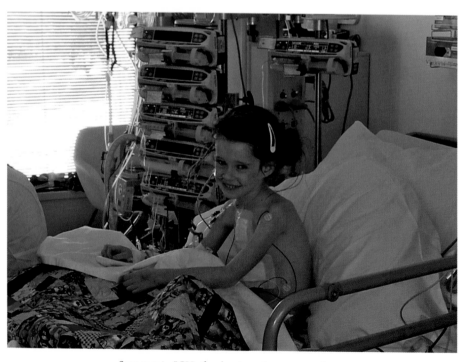

Summer in ICU after having a heart transplant.

Summer with Ralf and her parents, Samantha Brew and Chris Wilson, March 2014.

Ralf with Summer Wilson. He loves children . . . and ice-cream!

Lort Smith Animal Hospital and welfare centre.

Ralf (far right) with other Lort Smith volunteer dogs.

Caroline and Ralf with Melbourne's
Lord Mayor Robert Doyle at a fundraiser.
PICTURE: Emma Morgan

Liz Walker, Lort Smith CEO (from June 2010
to September 2014) with Esther.

Ralf with Archie ('Mini Ralf') and owner Annie Stillman at
The Royal Children's Hospital. PICTURE: Brenda Kittelty, RCH

Caroline Lovick with Ralf after winning the 2013 Lort Smith Volunteer Award.

Ralf with his Lort Smith volunteer bandana.

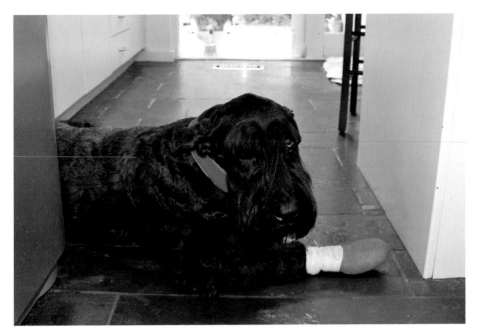

Ralf after his first operation in early 2014.

Claire Couwenberg reunited with Ralf in 2014, two years after he helped her walk again.

Ralf. September 2011.

the consent forms. Zeke was put on the waiting list for a liver. It was mid-2013.

Months later Jazmin was in Melbourne to appear in a fashion show. A pretty, elfin woman, she did a 'bit of modelling' from time to time. Her stepmother Annette, who lives near Jazmin, was looking after Jacob, Zeke and Sebastian while her stepdaughter stayed in the city overnight after the show. It was the first time in a while that Annette, who is close to the boys, had cared for them.

At six the next morning Annette awoke to the sound of pounding on her front door. She ignored it, hoping that whoever it was would go away, but the loud knocking continued. She stumbled to the door, barely awake, to see a policeman and a friend of Jazmin's standing behind him.

'What's happened to Jazmin?' she said.

'She's okay. Is Zeke Harrison here?' the policeman asked.

'Yes. Why?'

'There's a possible liver match for him—he needs to get to The Royal Children's Hospital as soon as possible. May I come in?'

Annette took the policeman through to the kitchen. Other members of the family appeared, bleary-eyed. The police officer asked Annette to gather anything that Zeke might need and the medication he was taking. Zeke needed to have his bottle before six-thirty and then fast from that time on, he said. The police officer phoned the transplant team to inform them he'd located Zeke and by six-thirty a dazed but ecstatic Annette was on the way to hospital with him, calling ahead to say she was nearby. She tried repeatedly to call Jazmin but her stepdaughter wasn't answering.

Jazmin had switched her mobile phone to 'silent' during the fashion show and had gone to the after-party with a friend. She stayed the night at her friend's house, and went to bed with the phone still on silent.

The length of time a 'harvested' liver can be stored outside the body has to be kept at a minimum to improve the new liver function. When doctors decide to go ahead with a donor retrieval they must be certain. The start time for preparing a recipient is strict—ideally less than six hours, although the organ can be left out up to twelve. If one child on the list isn't available, the transplant team organiser contacts the parents of another child. The medical team needs the written permission of the child's legal guardians to be able to perform the transplant.

Jazmin woke at seven o'clock, switched on her mobile phone and saw 178 missed calls. 'That can't be right,' she thought, pressing the first number that came up. A friend answered. 'They've found a liver for Zeke, you need to go to the hospital urgently, Zeke's already there with Annette.'

Without even pausing to listen to any more calls, Jazmin caught a taxi to the hospital, which was fortunately only fifteen minutes from where she was staying, arriving in Emergency shortly after Annette and the boys. She signed the necessary permission forms. Corey had also received several urgent calls from the hospital and was getting organised to head to Melbourne straight away.

A three-hour wait followed as Zeke was X-rayed and tested; at the same time, retrieval surgery for the donor liver was beginning, and the retrieval team was checking that it was healthy and suitable to use. Jazmin was so overwhelmed by emotions surging from hope to fear that she worried she would faint.

She called Corey, who was already on his way from Wyche-proof, so he could speak to his son before Zeke was prepped for surgery. Zeke was washed in a special bath then put on an intravenous drip for the anaesthetic. As they waited in the pre-operating room, Jazmin sang to Zeke. Just before he went under she cuddled him and said, 'You're not going to be sick anymore.' Zeke told his mother he loved her then drifted off.

The operation started at noon and was expected to take seven hours. But joining Zeke's bile ducts proved difficult and the surgery dragged on into the night. The surgeon emerged after twelve hours to say the liver transplant had been successful and that Zeke was recovering. Those were the most agonising twelve hours of his parents' lives—and then joy. 'The most amazing feeling ever,' says Jazmin.

Her first question was, 'What about his MSUD?'

'What MSUD?' said the surgeon, with a smile. 'He doesn't have it anymore.'

At 2.30 a.m., Jazmin and Corey were allowed in to see their son. Zeke was asleep in ICU, ventilated, his chest puffy with a big patch of bloodied gauze on it, tubes and wires everywhere. But he was cured. Three days later, as the drugs began wearing off and he awoke, Zeke looked up at his father and said, 'I feel a bit sick, Dad.' Corey choked up with pride at the courage his son had shown. Jazmin looked at their little boy and thought of the gift Zeke had received from the loved ones of another person who had just died. She would be forever thankful.

Zeke made headlines, becoming the first MSUD patient in Australia to receive a liver transplant. He remained in the hospital for more than three weeks after that. Jazmin stayed at Ronald McDonald House—the nearby retreat for families of children with serious illness—while Corey bunked down with a friend. Jazmin and Corey took turns to look after Zeke.

Jazmin began a new regime of medications when Zeke came home. He would be on anti-rejection medication for his liver for the rest of his life and there would be other restrictions, such as being unable to attend day care or kindergarten for six months after the transplant because of the risk of infection. He would continue to have blood tests but the regularity of these would decrease with time.

After the transplant Zeke changed. 'He's a completely new kid,' said Jazmin. 'Very energetic. He wants to chat to everyone and play on everything. He won't stop talking. His whole character has changed—he's a crazy little bubbly boy.'

The gastric tube is gone. He can now eat everything except grapefruit, which affects the way his body processes his anti-rejection drugs. There are no more frightening seizures, no more lengthy hospital admissions, no more pain. He learns more quickly.

'I knew his quality of life would be so much better with a transplant,' says his determined mother. She adds that she's a better person for all the hardship of Zeke's early life, more keenly aware of the goodness of others and the importance of loved ones.

As for Ralf, Zeke saw him again in the corridor one day some months afterwards, ran up to him and hooked his arm around him like an old buddy. Zeke was too young at the time of Ralf's visits to be able to remember him, but for some time after the visits he'd light up and say 'dog-dog' whenever Jazmin showed him *that* famous photo.

21

FAME

Ralf was already well-known by the time he met Zeke Harrison. He was the treasured acquaintance of hundreds of children and their parents, the much-loved friend of dozens of elderly folk and their families, his image stored on countless mobile phones and cameras of patients and relatives in Australia and overseas. Doctors and executives who visited The Royal Children's Hospital from other countries, never failed to be fascinated by him, often asking for photos with Ralf and no doubt relaying his story to colleagues at home.

The *Herald Sun* article published on 20 March 2012 about the 'giant miracle worker' made Ralf famous, and was retold many times all over the world.

On the morning it appeared, a friend of Lynda Tyzack rang

her to say that she'd seen a newspaper article about a Giant Schnauzer working as a therapy dog at The Royal Children's Hospital. 'Is he one of yours?' she asked.

'Of course! That's my Ralf!' Lynda exclaimed.

'I wasn't the least bit surprised that he'd be that good,' she says now, proudly.

Jenny Moore was in the supermarket in Perth, northern Tasmania, that morning and glanced down at a pile of the day's *Herald Sun* newspapers to see a photo of a Giant Schnauzer on the cover. She picked up a copy, peered closer and recognised Ralf. 'I got all excited! I was pleased that he was doing something good and was successful—his owners deserve a lot of credit for that.'

The Lovick family received countless emails in the week after the story appeared. Ralf became a local celebrity of sorts. The owner of Caroline's favourite cafe in Kew posted the article about him on the wall near the counter. Strangers in the street stopped to ask her if he was *the* Ralf in the photo. Caroline's hairdresser invited her to bring Ralf to the salon and the customers all patted and fussed over him when she did. The mother who coordinated the parent-teacher association at Camberwell Grammar, Ed's school, suddenly understood why Caroline could never attend meetings or help out on Mondays, the new day of her weekly hospital visits. Ed's hockey friends looked at Ralf anew when Caroline turned up to practice with him. Alice and Imogen followed the interest in Ralf when spending time on Facebook.

Many more people read the story on The Royal Children's Hospital website. Caroline became aware that even more parents were making appointments for their children at the hospital on Mondays. Not long after the story came out, she overheard a woman there remark to the mother standing next to her, 'I told you Ralf's here', as if he were a bona fide celebrity.

Ralf's story was reproduced in newspapers in the United Kingdom, the *Daily Mail* and *Sun* among them, and *The Huffington Post*, and then dispersed globally on all kinds of websites. Ralf was mentioned on sites based in Europe, India and Chile. He was popular on Spanish-speaking animal websites, *Tu Amigo el Perro* (Your Friend the Dog), *El Mundo Animal* (The World of Animals), and *Schnauzi*, a pet lovers' website. The story appeared on Petsetter, The Dog Journal, PawNation, Dogstuff and DogHeirs; as well as mainstream sites, from Pinterest and Pintrest'e (the Turkish version), Indulgy (a shopping site), to the Big Wife Health and Diet Blog. The Didyouknow blog on Tumblr had screens of 'likes' and 'reblogs' about Ralf.

Shortly after the story was published, a German radio crew contacted Caroline through hospital staff asking if they could travel to Melbourne to record a breakfast show about Ralf doing his rounds. *He's a dog, how will they manage that?* she wondered. The crew, who all spoke perfect English, followed Ralf and Caroline round the wards and took photos, presumably to post on the radio station's website.

Stories of Ralf spread all over Facebook, Twitter and other social media. Jazmin Hall saw the photo of Zeke and Ralf on Dawn French's Facebook page and thought, 'There's my baby!'

Three red dog tags engraved with Ralf's name arrived at Brenda Kittelty's office. They were sticky-taped to a letter from Karla of Donegal, Ireland, requesting Brenda pass them on to Caroline for Ralf.

In July 2013, sitting together below a large overhead TV in the lounge room, residents at Trinity Manor watched as Ralf and Caroline appeared on Channel Nine's *Today* show. 'That's our Ralf!' they said, chuffed.

Ralf became a pin-up boy at the Lort Smith. 'The unofficial face of pet therapy,' as volunteer coordinator Megan Nutbean puts it. 'He's definitely our most famous pet therapy dog. Everyone knows Ralf! Even people who have nothing to do with pet therapy know Ralf.' Megan, an ever-enthusiastic young woman with a distinctive crop of dark spirally hair, had heard of Ralf before she started working at the Lort Smith. She recalls how she has been in the reception area and watched pet owners walk in and recognise Ralf from articles they've read or the video he appears in on the Lort Smith website.

More than two years later, the photo of Ralf and Zeke is still cropping up in far-flung places. The Grace United Church in Caledonia, Ontario, Canada, ran a small story on Ralf in its March 2014 newsletter. When another picture of him was posted on The Royal Children's Hospital Facebook page in July 2014, dozens of grateful mothers, fathers and grandparents, posted messages.

The Lovick family took it all in their stride although Sam took to calling Ralf 'The Talent'. 'Oh, so The Talent's going to the vet!' he would say. But apart from that, Ralf was still the dog who'd hog the bed when you were trying to sleep in it or spread out on the lounge room couch when there was someone wanting to sit on it. Ralf was still just Ralf.

22

'THERE'S A DOG IN INTENSIVE CARE!'

One Thursday night in mid-May 2012, Caroline answered the door, amid the pounding of paws and a chorus of gruff barking, to the father of one of Ed's school friends, Henry. It was nearly nine-thirty and Henry's father was dropping Ed home. Caroline had never met Johnny Millar before, though she'd talked to his wife Julianne about the dance classes Ed and Henry were attending.

'I had to come and meet your dog,' Johnny said. He spoke with a soft Irish lilt but there was a tone of resolve in his voice.

Ralf was famous by now—it was about six weeks after the newspaper story had been published—but Caroline was surprised at the request. She found out later that Ed had taken a clipping of the story to school to show his Year 10 classmates.

Johnny explained that his son Henry, who loves dogs, had mentioned that the Lovicks had two 'amazing' Giant Schnauzers, one of which was a therapy dog that worked at The Royal Children's Hospital. Johnny worked in the hospital's Paediatric Intensive Care Unit.

Caroline showed him into the lounge as Ralf and Ivy careered around him.

'I need to ask you a favour,' he said. 'I want to organise for your dog to visit the ICU.'

Johnny explained that he had a patient, a boy, who was on heart bypass. 'I'd like to give him something that will make him cheery,' he said. He added that until Henry had told him about Ralf, he'd only been vaguely aware that there were therapy dogs elsewhere in the hospital.

'I thought dogs weren't allowed in the ICU?' said Caroline.

'I don't see why not.'

'Well, there's your therapy dog,' said Caroline, pointing to the over-excited Ralf.

Johnny had an expression on his face that said 'not *that* dog!' He'd been surprised too by the fierce, frenzied barking at the door. 'It was like the Hound of the Baskervilles,' he recalls, referring to the famous Sherlock Holmes story.

As he sat on the Lovicks' black leather lounge talking to Caroline, he had trouble imagining the galumphing animal in an ICU, squeezed in among all the electronic equipment, between all the tubes and drip stands. It was hard enough for people to negotiate, let alone a dog—and a huge hairy dog at that. Still, Johnny thought of the boy and stuck to his request.

'Intensive care can be overwhelming if you're not used to it,' he said to Caroline. 'The last thing I want is for you to be stressed.'

Without hesitation Caroline replied, 'I'll do it, but you'll have to get the clearance for it and jump through all the hoops.'

'I'll see what I can do and then let you know when I'd like you to come in,' said Johnny, thanking her as he left.

The Royal Children's Hospital ICU looks after critically ill children, from newborns to young adults, who have a severe condition, have experienced trauma or are in hospital for emergency or elective surgery. In this part of the hospital, the patients need invasive monitoring, intensive therapies and may be on life support. There are children on breathing machines, others who have kidney disease and are on dialysis, and some who are recovering from surgery and are heavily sedated.

Johnny Millar, a fit fifty-year-old, is the Head of Cardiac Intensive Care. He worked in ICU at the Royal Children's for eight years intermittently from 1996, then permanently from 2004, specialising in cardiac health. The hospital is the largest paediatric cardiac centre in Australia and the sole paediatric heart transplant centre. Johnny does his daily ward rounds along with the nurses, pharmacists, paediatricians and junior doctors, conducting examinations, writing treatment plans for the patients, dealing with new arrivals and making referrals. He takes readings from myriad monitors: heart rate, blood pressure, breathing rates, blood oxygen levels, fluid retention rates, monitors displaying IV drip solutions and so on—a wide range of complex information to process.

'But it's about the whole patient—not being distracted by the machines—and what they're telling you,' Johnny says. 'As you come to know the child and their family, you realise what's important to them, and what might make their time in hospital a bit easier.'

And sometimes that is a loved pet the child is missing.

Johnny admits that Ralf wasn't the first dog to come into his unit. 'We've smuggled in pets several times in the past,' he says, with a chuckle. 'It was usually Saturday or Sunday afternoon in the old hospital when it was quiet and there weren't too many people around who might object.'

Johnny, and other staff, would get the parents to spirit the dog into the hospital along the corridor to the helipad, then sneak it into intensive care, where he'd find them a room where the child could spend some time with their pet. The pets included a couple of small fluffy dogs that could sit on the lap of the sick child, and a big one that was more exuberant.

Most people associate ICU with acute care and short stays, but some children, perhaps those with chronic conditions or who are recovering from a bad accident, are there for weeks or even months.

'They lie there and it's a boring environment,' Johnny explains. 'There's only so much entertainment they can get on an iPad after a while.'

Visiting school teachers help, providing a link with something outside the hospital that the children associate with better times. Local celebrities including AFL football players, generous with their time, add a spark to a child's stay. The ICU staff sometimes wheel children outside in their beds or wheelchairs so they can smell the air and feel the sun on their skin, and do whatever else they can think of to make the child's stay happier. The hospital as a whole tries hard to keep its patients happy and entertained, with visits from 'clown doctors' and 'Starlight Captains' from the Starlight Foundation, which also runs an activity room. A giant man made of green and purple balloons might suddenly appear in a corridor or the doors of a child's room decorated by staff with a Happy Birthday message and cheerful paper cut-outs of little people.

Johnny is often struck by the resilience of very ill children and what they endure to recover. He says, though, that he enjoys the hurdles associated with working with them: 'It's academically and technically challenging, and physically and emotionally challenging, too.'

Meeting a child again after they've been discharged and have returned to say hello or have a check-up is a real source of joy. 'We often don't get a sense of what happens to them afterwards so one of our greatest rewards is seeing a family bring their healthy child back in after they've spent a long period of time here or have been extremely ill,' he says, adding, 'That really puts a smile on the faces of the nurses!'

Four days after Johnny Millar's visit, Caroline came across him in a lift at the hospital. This time Ralf was in full working mode, and so was Caroline—she exchanged a few words with Johnny, then, as the lift doors drew back, said, 'Can't chat now,

I'm working,' and quickly strode off down the corridor with Ralf, thinking only later that her rapid departure must have seemed rather rude. Within seconds, though, she and Ralf were surrounded by four or five children, like bees to a honey pot. She noticed Johnny watching Ralf as he walked past. He told her later he was amazed at the transformation in Ralf's demeanour from the dog he'd seen at her home. 'Caroline had described it but I wasn't prepared for just how dramatic a change it was,' he says.

That week Caroline received a call from Johnny saying he'd spoken to the boy's family—who were keen—and had cleared Ralf's visit with all the right people at the hospital. Could Ralf and Caroline visit ICU, Rosella ward, the following Monday? 'But I won't be there,' he added, 'I'm on a different shift.' He explained that Caroline and Ralf should wait outside the unit until Kristy Dea, one of the care managers, met them at the door to let them in and make them welcome. Someone would be with them the entire time, he assured Caroline.

Johnny had talked to his ICU colleagues about introducing a dog to the ward, asking if they had any problems with the idea, but all of them were happy about the prospect, as they, too, believed it would benefit the children. Some of them said they thought dogs weren't allowed in the unit. 'It was a perception,' says Johnny. 'As far as I knew there was no reason why they couldn't. Simple hygiene is all you need. We're very protective about children with compromised immune systems but most children in ICU have relatively normal immune systems.'

So at ten o'clock on Monday morning, Caroline and Ralf fronted up at ICU as arranged. She felt uncertain about how the visit to the gravely ill boy would play out but she reminded herself, 'I have my ace—Ralf!'

They were greeted in the corridor outside the unit by Kristy Dea, who swiped them through the stainless-steel doors. Kristy stressed, as Johnny had done, that someone would be with them the whole time.

People popped out of rooms to gawp at Ralf as the three of them walked down the corridor towards the boy. Doctors and nurses followed. *Like the pied piper. This is such a big deal!* thought Caroline, wishing that Johnny himself was there to witness it.

By the time they reached the child's room, a dozen or more staff had assembled just inside the doorway to watch the event. The room was crowded with people; the boy's parents stood to one side, looking expectant, with a brigade of doctors and nurses about a metre away from the bed, shifting around for a better position.

The boy, who looked to be about eight, was braced in a bed that was bent like a seat, his head supported by a pillow. All around there were cables, tubes and beeping machines. Caroline glanced at the tubes flowing with blood running from the boy's chest to a white plastic pump about the size of a baseball, a gentle sucking sound emanating from it.

Caroline and Kristy exchanged encouraging looks before Caroline stepped forward. 'Hi, this is Ralfie,' she said to the boy. 'Do you want to see Ralfie?'

The boy could barely move, he had little muscle control left, but he stirred slightly. Then the corners of his mouth curled up a little as he watched the approaching dog. Ralf walked up, put his head down lightly on the boy's lap and looked up at him through tufts of eyebrows. The boy contemplated the big furry head covering his legs, and touched Ralf's coarse hair, his face lighting up as he did. He turned to the people watching him, and smiled.

Cameras and smart phones clicked continuously. Everyone in the room seemed to be taking photos, rolling videos, with one of the doctors capturing images on the parents' camera. There were photos of the parents with their son and Ralf, then one of the boy and his father, the boy and his mother, the boy and Ralf, and finally the boy, Ralf and staff members. The boy was laughing.

Parents of other children came up to the door behind the doctors and nurses, craning their necks over shoulders to see what was going on.

Kristy kept an eagle eye on the proceedings, catching Caroline's eye now and then. After a while Caroline noticed that the boy was struggling to stay awake. 'Are you tired, honey? Shall I take Ralf out for a walk for a while?'

He started to nod off. She said goodbye as he gave Ralf a final pat. Caroline told him they'd see him next time.

But next time the boy was gone.

When Caroline walked out into the corridor, she wanted to cry and scream at the world, at the fickleness of disease and death. Instead, she focused on the boy's smiling face, on the joy that would be forever captured in those photos.

Johnny Millar's plan had worked.

Caroline prepared herself mentally to carry on with her visit. As the spectators started to disperse and the happy buzz of voices in and outside the room subsided, several other doctors approached Caroline to ask her if she and Ralf could visit *their* patients later. But as she and Ralf were making their way out of ICU, a nurse drew Caroline aside rather urgently. The nurse explained that the mother of a girl who was about to go on heart bypass had seen Ralf in the corridor and asked if he could visit her daughter, too.

'Of course,' said Caroline.

The nurse showed them into the next room where a tired but smiling woman stood beside the bed of a pig-tailed little girl. The girl was thin, pale, her face dull. Propped up in a squatting position in her pink kitty pyjamas, she stared down at the bed as if preoccupied. A tangle of tubes and wires, attached to all sides of her body, was connected to the bank of machines behind her.

'This is Summer,' the girl's mother said to Caroline as she led Ralf into the room.

Caroline tried hard not to take in the girl's name as she introduced herself and Ralf. Forgetting a child's name is a coping mechanism, she explains, though she recalls faces. If a child dies and she remembers their name, it weighs heavily.

All Ralf saw at the time was a girl he wanted to visit. His tail started to wiggle. *How close can I get to her? Can I get on her bed?*

The nurse helped Caroline lower the bed as far down as it would go so that Ralf could rest his front legs on it. Ralf looked intently at Summer. She reached out towards him, and although Ralf wasn't allowed to do it, he gave her hand a little lick.

'Take a photo!' Caroline urged the young girl's father, thinking back to the boy she had just visited. As he took the snapshot Summer inched her hand along the bed to feel Ralf's paw. She struggled to smile.

Her parents, Samantha and Chris, were overwhelmed.

'Before Ralf came, nothing positive had happened, everything was bad, really shitty,' says Chris. 'Seeing the joy on Summer's face made us forget what was going on, it was like a little breakthrough. It was like hope.'

A visiting emergency paediatrician walked into the room, saw the dog with his front paws on the bed and exclaimed, 'There's a dog in ICU!' Someone pulled him aside and told him about Ralf.

'Can you come in again?' Samantha asked, as Caroline prepared to leave with Ralf.

Caroline explained that she would need to get permission for Ralf to enter the unit but agreed to visit the following Monday if allowed. She was happy that Ralf had brought some pleasure into the little girl's life, and she silently hoped that she would see her again.

23

SUMMER'S STORY

Summer Wilson was born a beautiful baby with a perfectly round head, a little button nose and bow mouth. Delivered by emergency caesarean on 7 November 2006, in Redland Hospital, Brisbane, she was the first child of Chris Wilson and Samantha Brew, who had lived together for three years and, like any expectant parents, were thrilled by the birth of a healthy baby. Sam laughs as she recalls the little 'mohawk' of hair that Summer came into the world with.

When Summer was three, in late 2009, the family made a tree change to the tiny village of Tyalgum, near Murwillumbah, New South Wales. Chris and Sam bought a house on 20 hectares of land in wet eucalypt forest, clearing some of it to grow vegetables, raise chickens and produce as much of their own food as they could. Chris was a 'fly in, fly out' worker at mines in Western Australia; Sam, who'd left a council job in Brisbane, became a stay-at-home mother. Summer, a vivacious little girl with long brown hair, started at kindergarten at the local primary school.

But early the following year, five-year-old Summer became ill; vomiting, lethargic and not eating. Sam suspected a virus and took her to their local doctor. After examining her, the doctor said that based on Summer's symptoms, it was a stomach virus. Sam talked to other parents but none of them reported any tummy 'bugs' going round at the time, which she thought was curious.

Summer was still vomiting a week later. The doctor's surgery was closed at the time so Sam took her to the hospital at Murwillumbah where she was seen by a doctor in Emergency. Summer laughed and chatted happily to the nurses as she perched on the bed waiting to be treated. The doctor prescribed hydrolytes and sent them home.

Two days later Summer was still unwell and Sam noticed that her feet had become puffy. She was surprised that her daughter hadn't recovered by now; Summer had always been a healthy child. She made an appointment with the local doctor that morning. This time the doctor suggested taking her to the hospital.

Summer was examined at Murwillumbah hospital by a female doctor, a South African woman who seemed 'sharp'. She had the little girl X-rayed and, as she analysed the scan, she turned to Sam and Chris and said, 'Your daughter has fluid in pretty much all her cavities—lungs, heart, abdomen, they're all full of fluid. And she's got an enlarged heart.'

Sam and Chris were dumbfounded, disbelieving, then a flood of questions poured out: *How could this happen? How could she be that bad? Why?*

The doctor explained that fluids had built up because Summer's heart wasn't pumping blood properly. 'She needs to go to Tweed Heads hospital straight away.'

Within minutes Summer was strapped to a stretcher and in an ambulance, lights on and sirens blaring. Sam sat in the back of the ambulance with her; Chris followed in the family car.

At the Tweed Hospital, Summer, by now looking lethargic, was examined again and underwent an ultrasound. She was given diuretic injections to help her expel the fluids building up in her body. She wee'd and wee'd and wee'd, says Chris, and finally she started to feel better.

But as Sam sat in the emergency room with their daughter, Chris was taken outside into the corridor by one of the paediatric specialists.

'Get all your family and friends in here,' he said. 'Her heart is failing—it's only pumping at 10 per cent capacity.'

Chris felt like he'd been hit with a baseball bat.

He staggered back into the room. Summer was sitting on the bed, making the doctors around her laugh, giggling herself. It was surreal.

Chris didn't ring any relatives right then. He couldn't. Nor did he repeat the doctor's words to Sam.

Another paediatric specialist was making arrangements for Summer to be sent to Brisbane, taking a video of the ultrasound on his iPhone and sending it ahead. A doctor phoned Chris's sister Angela, who lived near the Sunshine Coast, to let her know what was happening. It took Chris another hour to be able to call his parents and Sam's mother to convey the news, to be able to get the words out. His world was becoming a nightmarish blur.

A transfer team of two cardiac specialists from Brisbane's Mater Children's Hospital soon arrived by taxi, carrying with them the specialised equipment they needed to transfer Summer safely to the hospital. Sam and Summer were put into another ambulance and arrived at the Mater hospital emergency department at 11.30 p.m., where Summer was immediately wheeled into the Paediatric ICU. The director of the unit looked at the ultrasound and turned to Chris and Sam. 'This isn't good,' he said.

Yet there was still no diagnosis.

The couple stayed in Summer's room in ICU that night, Sam barely sleeping as she sat upright resting her head on Summer's bed, Chris managing just a few fitful hours.

The following day Summer was wheeled into the cardiac ward where doctors started tests using a range of drugs to assess which ones she would respond to best. Sam stayed with Summer in hospital each night, sleeping on a divan bed next to her daughter; Chris slept at his parents' home while they waited for the results.

'There were mixed messages from the doctors,' he recalls. 'The main doctor was cheery but he didn't give us false hopes; they still couldn't find out what was wrong with her heart.'

Over the next two weeks the doctors tried a suite of drugs but still there was no improvement or explanation. Summer's health was declining. She'd lost a lot of weight and was now being tube-fed. Her digestive system was shutting down, as were other parts of her body.

Eventually, one of the cardiologists called Chris and Sam into an interview room and sat down with them.

'There are three ways this can go,' he said. 'Think of thirds. The top third is the best outcome—it's a virus and the patient can go home. Then there's the middle third where we can manage the condition on drugs. Then there's the end third and that's a bad outcome.'

Summer had an MRI scan to further investigate what was happening to her heart. Chris and Sam were told that the scan was vital for making a diagnosis but that it carried a huge risk— Summer might not survive the general anaesthetic needed to keep her sedated and still while she was in the machine.

But she did survive, and afterwards the cardiologist came back to Sam and Chris with the results. 'Not only is she in the bad third, but she's at the bad end of the bad third,' he said.

The only hope for Summer was a heart transplant. However, he warned them that waiting for a heart that may never arrive or may be rejected after the operation could be a devastating process. 'You may not want to consider doing it,' he added.

Of course, we'll do it, thought Chris. *We'll do anything.*

This was the first time the idea of a heart transplant had been raised with Chris and Sam. It was less than a month since Summer had first fallen ill, now she needed someone else's heart to survive—it was hard to keep up with all that was happening.

The cardiologist explained that Summer needed to get to The Royal Children's Hospital in Melbourne. Arrangements had to be made immediately. She would leave on a Royal Flying Doctor Service (RFDS) flight in three days with Sam, while Chris organised the belongings they would need for what could be an extended stay in Melbourne. The couple was told another family had stayed in Melbourne for a year while they were waiting for a donor for their child.

Chris returned home to pack up their lives, helped by his sister Angela and her husband. They selected the clothing they thought the family would need for a year then vacuum-sealed the rest of it. They cleared out the fridge and gave the food to the chickens. The chooks would go to Sam's mother, while Chris's parents looked after the dogs, Titan the Rottweiler, and Pawprint the Blue Heeler. Chris did the 'thousand other things' that needed to be done to move house in a hurry, closed the front door and drove to his parents' home in Brisbane. The following day, he set off on the long drive to Melbourne.

Summer was flown from Brisbane to Essendon Airport then transferred by ambulance to The Royal Children's Hospital. As there were no free beds in the ICU, she was taken to a general ward where she was connected to various machines and monitored constantly. Sam recalls a lot of 'to-ing and fro-ing' as a stream of cardiac specialists, surgeons, doctors and nurses came in and out of the room, hovering around their daughter, often speaking to each other in whispered tones.

Sam had been up since 3.30 a.m. and the grinding anxiety was taking its toll on her. 'I felt hammered,' she confides. She and Summer remained in the cardiac ward for a while, during which time Sam was given a meal by the nurses, a kind gesture, and met the Paediatric Cardiac Transplant Coordinator, Anne Shipp.

That night, the doctors told Sam they were transferring Summer into the ICU. 'I'm coming with her!' she told them. 'I'll stay on the floor.' The doctors assured Sam she could stay with her daughter and that the ICU had fold-out divans.

Chris arrived the next day and there were more discussions with the transplant team. Summer's parents were told by a female medico that their daughter would be put on a Ventricle Assistance Device (VAD), a machine that would take over the beating of her heart while she waited for a donor heart to become available. The hospital only had one of these at the time and it was being used for another patient, so another VAD was being flown in from Germany. Sam and Chris glanced at each other, alarmed; it all sounded so drastic. There was only a two-in-three chance of survival associated with the VAD, they were told.

Summer was being closely monitored but her health was still deteriorating. She was exhausted, unable to sleep for long because of the way she was propped up in bed attached to the many machines, but she was at least able to share a joke with Sam about a mask strapped to her face that made her look like a fighter pilot. Two days later, she was due to be connected to the VAD, which had been delayed in arriving. Sam and Chris were looking forward to the process moving on but were dreading it, too, anxious about the operation that would stop Summer's own heart from functioning and unnerved by the idea that their daughter's life would then depend on the machine. Their lives seemed to lurch from one crisis to the next.

Two days before the operation was due to take place, Sam, drawn out and anxious, walked out of Summer's room into the corridor and spotted an enormous black dog.

'Oh my god!' she exclaimed. 'It's a dog!' Amid all the gloves, gowns, masks, machines, procedures and sterility—a dog! She felt instantly, unaccountably elated.

She quickly approached the closest nurse. 'What's that dog doing in here?' she asked.

The nurse explained that Ralf was a therapy dog who was here to visit a very sick boy.

'Can he see my daughter, too?' Sam couldn't get the words out fast enough.

Soon afterwards, Caroline and Ralf entered the room where he was to meet Summer for the first time. Summer was well used to big dogs—she had Titan the Rottweiler at home—but this one 'looked like a big horse', she recalled later. She noticed that he had the same collar as Titan, 'real soft paws', and a beard she wanted to brush. 'He wanted to get up on the bed, his back legs were going like he was on tippy toes.'

The day Summer was due to undergo her VAD operation came around quickly. The operation was scheduled for 11.30 a.m. But at nine that morning the transplant team approached Sam and Chris. The operation had been cancelled: Summer was to have a heart transplant instead.

In an extraordinary twist of fate, a donor heart had just become available.

Chris and Sam stared at the doctor in disbelief. They weren't even aware that Summer had been put on the transplant waiting list. In a world in which their lives were being rolled around by fate, Summer had just won the lottery.

The heart transplant commenced at 11 that morning. Sam and Chris were instructed to leave the hospital, to go and do something that would take their minds off the operation. The doctors told them it would take four hours and was what they called a 'dumb' operation because it was relatively simple to perform. But a patient had a 5- to 10-per-cent risk of not surviving, and because Summer's heart was already failing, that risk had increased to 20 per cent. 'We'll know more once we have the heart going,' the surgeon told Sam. The doctors still had no idea what had caused Summer's heart to deteriorate. It was still operating at 10 per cent of normal capacity.

So Sam, Chris and Angela went out for lunch at a nearby pub. 'Angela's a nurse and very positive. It was good to have an extra person there,' says Sam.

At three o'clock they received the call from the hospital: the operation had gone well and they could go in to see Summer at five. The relief for them was overwhelming.

Still, Sam and Chris were shell-shocked when they saw their daughter, sedated yet writhing a little as she tried to tug at the wires attached to her and the tube in her mouth. Everyone they'd spoken to at the hospital had always been direct about the risks and what could happen at any stage—an approach Sam and Chris appreciated—but it barely softened each blow.

Sam and Chris had been told early on that they, and Summer, would receive counselling to help them understand and cope with the transplant process. 'But because the donor heart became available so quickly, there was no time for counselling,' explains Sam. 'We picked it up on the fly.'

Ultimately the doctors weren't able to find the cause of Summer's illness beyond describing it as 'idiopathic dilated cardiomyopathy', a general term for heart failure with no discernible cause, which they explained was probably congenital.

'There was no relief—we felt like we'd just entered into a long haul,' says Sam. 'Plenty could still go wrong.'

Summer was fragile, so thin the skin hung off her bottom. Aside from the risk that her body could reject the donor heart, Summer's immune system would always be compromised, and she would be more prone to cancer and viruses.

But she was alive.

The Monday after the operation Caroline Lovick edged her head through the opened door to Summer's room to check whether she was there and if she felt up to seeing a couple of visitors. She was pleased to see Summer in the room with Chris, recognisable behind his gown and mask; she'd dreaded an empty bed. A nurse greeted Caroline but asked her not to come in: Summer was on immune suppressants because she'd had a heart transplant and could easily pick up an infection.

A heart transplant? Caroline could barely believe that this was the same little girl they'd met only a week ago. She quickly stepped back from what she now realised was a sterile room, but just as she did Ralf pushed past her and stuck his nose through the gap in the door.

Summer was sitting up cross-legged in bed, her chest bandaged above the jagged red line running down her torso. She looked up from her bed and laughed. It was the first time she'd smiled in three weeks. 'Ralf, look at my scar!'

Before he could accept the invitation, Caroline hauled Ralf back, saying to Summer, 'You be a good girl and we'll come back soon!'

Caroline's joy at seeing Summer was tempered with sadness as she later thought about the donor. *Some beautiful parents of a dying child have said yes to that transplant*, she thought. *And because of them, Summer's alive.* That night Caroline Lovick told her children over dinner that they were all signing up to become organ donors.

Summer stayed at The Royal Children's Hospital for two weeks after her heart transplant, moving to a general ward, slowly regaining her strength and gaining weight. Caroline visited her on her rounds, watching the patient she and Ralf were so fond of become stronger and cheekier.

But they missed a week on their rounds and during that time Sam, Chris and Summer moved out of the general ward and into Ronald McDonald House, coming into the hospital every week for blood tests to check her medication, the levels of her oxygen and white blood cell counts and so on, as well as biopsies to monitor her heart for signs of rejection. The closest Summer and Sam came to seeing Ralf was when Sam peered out the hospital window one day and saw the retreating figures of Caroline and Ralf walking through the parkland below.

Weeks later, as the time approached for the family to return home Summer made a present for Ralf—a toy dog fashioned from an empty water bottle coloured in black texta, with black straws for legs, and a tail. She and Sam also bought him a chewy toy, but, not being able to give them to Ralf personally, left the gifts at the Lort Smith nearby. Sam hoped that Caroline would get in touch after they received the gifts so they could meet up before they left for New South Wales.

But Summer's present wasn't passed on to Caroline for some time.

In a final bid to get in touch with her, Sam rang Brenda Kittelty to see if she could pass on Caroline's phone number. Brenda said that unfortunately she wasn't able to give out the numbers of volunteers, 'But you can see her if you like, she's here now.'

Sam and Summer walked across from Ronald McDonald House to find Caroline in reception waiting for them. Summer sprinted up to Ralf and hugged him. 'I'm so happy to see you, Ralf!'

The two women exchanged phone numbers and arranged to meet in the parkland the next time they were both at the hospital. That was the first of a series of play dates in the hospital grounds.

Sam, Chris and Summer were looking forward keenly to returning home, to having their dogs again, and getting the chickens back. For Summer, it would also mean seeing the friends she missed from school who'd sent her a folder of 'get well' messages and paintings they'd made. Sam's former work colleagues at the Redlands council had sent cards and messages, too, and had raised funds to help with Summer's medical needs. The family were able to buy a new car and took time out for a holiday on their way home. They went tobogganing in the Victorian snowfields—'I face-planted,' says Summer, very proudly—fossicked for gold at Sovereign

Hill, stopped at Bathurst in New South Wales—all a welcome release after what had seemed like a lifetime in hospital.

The family returned to Tyalgum where, as part of their 'rehabilitation', they tried to get back to normality as quickly as possible. Chris resumed his job in mining, although he stopped working in Western Australia. Summer went back to school with strict new instructions to wash her hands often and to never share food or pencils with other children in case of infection. Sam and Chris cleared more land for their vegetables and added more livestock.

Sam hovers near her only child more than she would have done previously, always making sure Summer wears sunscreen to guard against skin cancer and keeping her away from any sources of infection as far as possible. Summer has been admitted to hospital twice with gastric infections picked up at school. She has to take medication three times a day for the rest of her life, but is otherwise a healthy, happy child.

Summer still has play dates with Ralf whenever the family comes to The Royal Children's Hospital for check-ups, walking in Royal Park or other parks around the city. The adults chat as Summer wanders the lawns with Ralf at her side. Bystanders marvel at the sight of such a slight girl leading around such a hulking dog. Summer sometimes brings gifts for Ralf, perhaps a bracelet she's made out of beads for him to wear on a hairy leg. She's even allowed to feed him ice-cream. Caroline is now the one taking photos. 'If I'm ever having a crappy day, I look at those photos, see Summer's smile, and remember why I get out of bed!' she says.

24

CHILDREN TO REMEMBER

The relationships Caroline and Ralf formed with most of the children and parents they visited were fleeting. The pair dispensed moments of happiness and warmth during what was for most families a strange and worrisome time, then moved on to the next room. Yet the effects of their visits could be profound. 'Even a minute or two can make a difference,' says Caroline.

Then there were patients whom she and Ralf encountered on a number of occasions—children who were in for a long stay, those who'd turn up in outpatients for a follow-up consultation, and others returning for a different procedure. These were people she'd see over weeks or months and come to know in the way you might a distant cousin. A few, like Summer's family, became firm friends.

And there were children who, among the hundreds of patients Caroline and Ralf visited, would forever stand out in her mind.

Caroline recalls the time she and Ralf were asked to help an eight-year-old boy become mobile again. The boy had endured many operations and had no muscle control; he flopped like a rag doll. And he was in pain when he moved. The physiotherapy session would be difficult. One of the doctors, a woman, kneeled behind the boy on the bed, holding his head up; two other doctors flanked the boy and two more positioned themselves in front of him, one clasping him around the waist as a nurse stood behind that doctor to steady him. The physiotherapist was poised in front of the boy, ready to move his arms and legs, as Caroline and Ralf attracted his attention, distracting him from the pain he was about to feel. The boy's mother looked on. 'Ralf's here,' said Caroline. 'Ralfie's going to sit down. See!'

In a concerted movement they all raised the boy's body to a sitting position then shifted him to the edge of the bed. The boy, who had been on his back for months, looked nauseous. 'Ralfie's going to put his head on your lap now,' Caroline said. 'Is that okay, darling?'

The physiotherapist and Caroline then picked up the boy's feet and rested them on Ralf's head. 'Ooh, Ralfie likes that!' she observed. They rubbed his hands against Ralf's whiskers. And that was it for the day.

'All those adults holding up a kid so he could pat a dog!' Caroline says, laughing now.

But it was a vital start. And the sessions progressed, tiny movement by tiny movement.

Another volunteer Annie Stillman and her therapy dog Archie, a black Miniature Schnauzer, came in to see the boy on other days. Archie was sometimes paired with Ralf on a shift and became known as 'Mini Ralf'. Weeks later, the team took the boy for his first walk down the hallway. They all set off, the boy's arms leaning on the edge of a walker with Ralf's lead looped around it, one doctor supporting the boy's head, another his torso, everyone shuffling down the hallway in unison.

Three or four months later that boy was running down the corridor by himself to greet Caroline and Ralf—a sight she'll never forget.

Occasionally Caroline came across a young patient who seemed to have copped more than their share of hardship— these were the times she found most testing, when her carefully constructed emotional barriers were pushed to breaking point.

One teenage girl, a petite sixteen-year-old from rural Victoria, had just had surgery on her thigh when Caroline and Ralf first met her. To Caroline, she was like a 'little angel', blonde, softly spoken with sparkling eyes, her face a little puffy. The physiotherapists wanted to get her mobile again; if Ralf got on her bed she would have to shift over for him, moving of her own accord.

Caroline saw the girl again some time later—this time she'd had an organ transplant and was recovering from the operation in the surgical ward.

The next time they saw the girl, months later, she was in lock-down in ICU and very ill. She'd had four or five operations since they last met. Ralf was allowed in because he couldn't transmit any germs but Caroline had to stay on the other side of the door, extending the lead as far as it would go so he could reach her bed. This time the teenager could do little more than stroke Ralf once or twice. *Come on, someone cut her some slack!* Caroline thought.

Very occasionally she's caught completely unawares, her professional mask not in place. She will never forget Natasha, the girl she and Ralf saw over a number of months, who'd been severely burned. Natasha was bandaged like a mummy when they first visited her, with only a tiny tuft of dark blonde hair poking out. She'd been in the ICU for four weeks, her life sometimes in the balance. Natasha's mother Elizabeth says her daughter, seven at the time, was very depressed. She couldn't use her hands and was barely able to move the rest of her body. She hated the physiotherapy that caused her so much pain. Nobody could get through to her to make her smile, giggle or want to begin to move properly again, Elizabeth says. Yet Natasha always made the effort to turn her head when Ralf walked past.

During one particularly arduous physiotherapy session, Elizabeth's husband Brendan felt he needed a break, left the room, and saw Caroline and Ralf about to leave the hospital for the day. He begged Caroline to stay a little longer and to take Ralf in to see Natasha. Caroline agreed, with characteristic enthusiasm. She followed Brendan back towards the room; Natasha's cries could be heard from outside it. But as soon as Natasha saw Ralf she settled, broke into a smile, said hello and asked him how he was.

Burns patients are very sensitive because they've lost skin, are prone to infection and easily hurt, so Caroline and Ralf had to be particularly careful when they approached Natasha's bed. Caroline supported Ralf as he stood up by the side of the bed, gripping his hindquarters firmly to stop him slipping. Natasha looked into Ralf's eyes and talked to him some more—talking was all she *could* do. 'The only thing that lifted Natasha's spirits in hospital then was Ralf,' Elizabeth says.

Sometimes Natasha was well enough to see Ralf, at other times she was unconscious, or the family was too upset to take visitors. On occasions Elizabeth would come out of the room by herself for a pat.

On some of the early visits, Natasha could only move three fingers, extending them out of her clump of bandages to touch the fur on Ralf's toes. On a later visit one whole hand was free to stroke Ralf's head. Caroline grew fond of Natasha, who they would see every week, enjoying watching her gradual improvements. But as the girl recovered, Caroline lost touch with her for a while.

About nine months after they'd first met, Caroline was walking into the main entrance with Ralf, about to start work, when a long-haired girl ran through the corridor at her shouting 'Ralf!' then 'See, I told you, Mum!' and hugged the dog. It was Natasha, without the bandages, moving freely.

Caroline greeted Elizabeth, whom she did not immediately recognise, but Natasha was too excited to stop talking long enough to say hello. 'What time is it, Mum? Am I late for the appointment, can I walk Ralf?'

'Here you go, honey, you can take him for a walk,' Caroline said, handing Natasha the lead without looking at her. Then she turned to Natasha's mother, tears running down her face. 'She looks great.'

'I'm sorry, you weren't ready for that, were you?' Elizabeth asked.

Caroline listened intently as the mother told her of the progress Natasha had made, before continuing on her way into the hospital, warmed by the encounter. It was one of those times when life just sang.

There were other patients Caroline saw week after week, hoping each time for good news. She remembers one teenage girl who spent months in an ICU ward waiting for a kidney transplant. Each time Caroline visited her, the girl would wish aloud that she could be moved to the adolescent ward. Her whole aim in life was to be well enough to shift wards. The girl adored seeing Ralf but when she was really ill—and down— she didn't want to have anything to do with him. 'That's when I used to worry,' says Caroline.

Another patient, Coen Ashton, also stood out for his determination. He was born with cystic fibrosis, a life-threatening, genetically inherited disease that causes mucus to build up in the lungs and digestive system, making it a battle to breathe. In March 2011, Coen, with greatly diminished lung capacity, jet-skied 2000 kilometres down the Murray River—with his parents' blessing and support— to encourage Australians to pledge their organs. It took him seven weeks. More than 1000 people signed up to the Australian Organ Donor Register.

Six months later, Coen was put on the waiting list for a set of donor lungs and his family given two weeks to leave their home in Maryborough, Queensland, for Melbourne, where his treatment would begin at The Royal Children's. He was in isolation, hooked to an intravenous drip and sitting on the floor when he first met Ralf. This time, even Caroline looked surprised as Ralf entered the room and without hesitation walked straight over to Coen, flopping down next to him. 'Ralf turned up and made himself comfortable—like they'd been buddies forever,' says Coen's mother, Dawn.

Coen had seen therapy dogs before at the Royal Children's Hospital in Brisbane, where he'd been treated previously, but had never bonded with any of them, Dawn says. Ralf didn't sniff around the room looking for scraps of food as some of the other therapy dogs had done; his whole focus was on the young patient. Says Coen, 'There wasn't much else to look forward to. Ralf was special, he understood me and seemed to know I couldn't do much with him but sit there.'

Ralf and Caroline visited Coen a number of times in the following months as his health progressively worsened. The emotional strain of watching her son being bedridden took its toll on Dawn. Caroline remembers her saying, desperately, 'I can't bear it any more—I'm taking him out to ride on his scooter!'

Says Dawn, 'At the time you're trying to do your best for your child. That's your whole focus in life. You have to keep him motivated so he can stay well enough for long enough to live to find a suitable donor—the more days he spent without getting out of bed, the less likely it was that he was going to get out of bed.'

Ralf's visits played a big part in this. 'When you're at the end of the road and waiting for a transplant, there's really not much else a doctor can do. Ralf was doing more than the doctors could do. They should call him Doctor Ralf!' she jokes.

In late 2012, Coen was very ill and close to being put on life support when a pair of donor lungs became available. Since his transplant, Coen, now seventeen, has stepped up his efforts to encourage people to sign up and become organ donors, winning the Pride of Australia Medal for his work, and voluntarily gives presentations about cystic fibrosis at schools. He jet-skied down the Murray again in March 2014, this time in seven days.

The good-looking, mop-topped teenage boy is the public face of his campaign, but Dawn is a driving force behind it, says Caroline. 'He's got an awesome mother. It's often the mummies that move everything along,' she says. 'As they say, a desperate mother is better than the whole FBI. And the medical staff at the Royal Children's listen to them.'

Claire Couwenberg was a lively, independent little girl before doctors found a cancerous growth the size of a small football on her kidney in January 2012. The Wilms' tumour fortunately was treatable but the downside for Claire, and her parents Marie and Gene, was that she would have to undergo an arduous and, at times, painful sequence of treatments in the months ahead. Life for the two-and-a-half-year-old girl would become a sequence of tests, X-rays, biopsies, surgery, chemotherapy, radiotherapy, transfusions and other procedures.

Surgeons successfully removed the tumour on 14 March 2012. Five days later, Claire was taken off morphine and prescribed milder painkillers and had started to eat solid food again. But she wasn't coping well, Marie says. She seemed 'out of it', unsettled and unhappy. When a medical practitioner came into the room wanting to check her abdomen she'd glower, get upset and try to push them away. The doctors suggested that Marie and Gene gently encourage their daughter to get out of her wheelchair and get moving again; she refused. Claire would not walk.

Marie was about to wheel her daughter around the hospital as a diversion the day Caroline Lovick walked past them saying that she and Ralf were visiting people and would Claire like to see him? The family had a large dog at home, Benny the Bullmastiff-cross, who Claire was missing, so Marie said she was sure that she'd enjoy a visit from another dog. She turned to look at her daughter. Claire was fixated on Ralf, her whole demeanour transformed at the sight of him. She started smiling, saying 'Dogg-ie, dogg-ie' and pointing animatedly. When Caroline handed her Ralf's lead, she stood up, wobbled unsteadily on her feet as she got her balance—and walked. Marie moved quickly to stand behind her daughter to support her. She was astounded. 'She was so determined to walk with Ralf,' she says. 'Nothing else mattered to her— for a moment it was like she wasn't even sick. It made me so happy.'

Marie says meeting Ralf undoubtedly sped up Claire's recovery, and that it helped buoy her and her husband, too.

'It made us look at ourselves—if she can do it, we can get through this.'

A photograph of Claire appeared in the same newspaper article about Ralf as the one Zeke Harrison was in. It's now stuck on a wall at home, a reminder to Marie of the time from which she, Gene and their healthy five-year-old daughter have moved on, and of a kind gesture that meant more than Caroline Lovick could ever have imagined.

25

OFFICIAL DUTIES

There were a few telltale signs that something doggie was afoot in Carlton, inner-city Melbourne. People were drifting out of the gardens surrounding the Royal Exhibition Building carrying showbags with paw prints on them, clasping dog beds under their arms and wearing cardboard dog ears on their heads. Trailers outside the building were marked 'Caution: show dogs' and vans advertised Howling Husky Sled Dog Tours and The Wonderdogs.

The annual Dog Lovers Show at the Royal Exhibition Building in Melbourne is a big event on the dog enthusiast's calendar. Thousands of people attend it over the three days it's held in May and thousands more when it's staged later in Sydney. Ralf was appearing at the Lort Smith stand, where staff and volunteers were on hand to promote the work of the animal hospital, rattle tins to raise money and sell merchandise. Caroline had volunteered her and Ralf's services as representatives of the dog therapy program for a couple of hours on the last day.

Ralf was a drawcard whenever Lort Smith took its cause to the public; it was well known within the organisation that Caroline's tin was always heavier than the others at the end of the day. 'It's Ralf—he does that.' Once when they were collecting donations at Parliament Station, Caroline and Ralf filled three tins. Sometimes a tin will get so heavy that she'll swap it with someone else for a lighter one. People are generous when it comes to helping animals or children, she says, and often the ones who look least able to afford it give the most.

Caroline and Ralf arrived at the Dog Lovers Show after lunch. The Royal Exhibition Building was still packed, all around the hum of voices and the pump of music from a central arena. The building's vast timber floor was crowded with hundreds of stands offering canine-inspired merchandise and services. The arena was hosting action displays by dog troupes and a centre stage was devoted to talks and demonstrations by experts in health and handling. It was a friendly event where everyone had the same thing in common, where, like walks in the park, it was easy to strike up a conversation with a stranger. Caroline, having heard from a friend that the show was worth a visit, decided to wander around before taking up her position at the Lort Smith stand.

The Royal Exhibition Building is a grand affair, built in 1880 in the days of Marvellous Melbourne, when the city was fat with gold rush money. The domed building with its opulent interior, murals and huge semicircular stained-glass windows was Australia's largest building at the time. It hosted Melbourne's first international exhibition that year, and hundreds of trade shows, fairs, community and cultural events followed. Now there are wedding expos, beer festivals, classic car shows, art and antique fairs. The Dog Lovers Show came a week after a tattoo festival. Caroline found this out when she inadvertently went to the venue a week early. As she stopped to chat to people she wondered about the number of heavily tattooed visitors and the preponderance of chunky Staffordshire Terriers in studded collars and bandanas, before realising that she'd come in the wrong week.

At first glance the one thing that seemed in short supply at the Dog Lovers Show were *dogs*. The only canines allowed were special animals: performing dogs, prime examples of certain breeds, rescue dogs, service dogs like Ralf and working animals. There were sheep dogs, agility dogs, customs and border protection dogs, Chester 'the Famous Skateboarding Dog'. But visitors are banned from bringing their own pets. 'Not even little ones', said the information for show-goers.

The 'breed dogs' were on display in stands and pens on the gallery above the pavilion but there weren't many of them. Caroline and Ralf passed immaculately groomed Siberian Huskies, Bernese Mountain Dogs and snowy white Poodles that looked like they'd been topiaried. Several Old English Sheepdogs with combed fringes and silky locks waited patiently at the front of their stand, one with its hair fetchingly arranged in a topknot. Another two were so fluffy, so clean and so still they looked like giant soft toys—and on closer inspection, they were!

Caroline walked back to the stairs, passing the display for the Schnauzer Club, where a man was holding a Miniature Schnauzer, cute as a button, while talking to an interested couple. Later, she met a woman from that stand walking two Miniatures. She was in raptures at the sight of her first Giant Schnauzer.

Downstairs again, Caroline paused to marvel at the array of doggie goods and services, some of which she didn't know existed. There were stands advertising canine nannies and doggie day care, dog hotels, transport, training, bedding, traditional medicine for dogs, the latest in scientifically developed supplements, doggie health foods with spirulina, kale and antioxidants, beauty products for fur and nails, fashionable canine clothes, jewellery, gourmet vineyard tours, an 'animal whisperer' whose sign claimed she could communicate telepathically and intuitively with dogs, and someone offering 'dognitive therapy'. There was aromatherapy for the dogs and odour neutralisers for their owners. A section was devoted to rescue groups. The Pug SOS pen was particularly popular, with ten or so of the flat-faced dogs in their pale blue bandanas sitting panting on laps, in cages or on the floor. The dogs had been saved from becoming puppy factory bitches, someone explained to an onlooker. The stallholders smiled hopefully at the constant stream of passers-by, willing them to stop and talk, if not buy or sign up for something.

Caroline found the Lort Smith stand, greeted the two other volunteers collecting donations, volunteer coordinator Megan Nutbean and vet Russell Harrison. She positioned Ralf in the busy thoroughfare between the stands and got to work. A middle-aged man grappling with the depths of his pockets pulled out a handful of coins, fed them into the slit of the plastic can and asked if he could pat Ralf. 'Of course you can,' said Caroline. 'He's a trained therapy dog so it's almost compulsory!' People started gathering around them, changing places to get a closer look at Ralf's face, taking photos with their mobile phones, bending over to tell him how 'gorgeous' he was and asking Caroline questions about his work and the breed. Caroline answered all questions carefully and introduced Ralf to anyone who caught her eye, seemingly at ease with the process. Yet underneath she is always alert, on guard for unexpected behaviour, a young child that might poke Ralf in the eye, for instance.

All sorts of people paused to talk but as yet, no children. Ralf turned his head away from the crowd to look back into the Lort Smith stand; he knew there were treats in Caroline's bag on the floor behind him and could smell the goodies for sale on the table. 'No, we're not having chewies,' she told him. Attention back on the job, Ralf perked up at the sight of a young girl carrying a balloon shaped like a fat Beagle, her face skilfully painted to resemble the dog's, with a sprinkling of glitter thrown in for good measure. She hung around, chubby fingers kneading the top of Ralf's head, trying to read the words on his bandana, intrigued by him—'Ralf's really nice!'—until her mother pulled her away and onto the next stand. At the holistic dog food stand next door people were blocking the aisle queuing for free showbags. Many people were carrying bags containing samples of dry feed or free treats, and passing by tantalisingly close to Ralf's nose. A boy with a polystyrene tray of chips approached, almost at face height. Ralf couldn't help himself; he almost drooled.

'Is he allowed a treat?' a woman asked.

'Not while he's working,' Caroline replied, explaining a little about the therapy dog program.

As she did so, a young couple waited patiently for Caroline to finish talking to the woman to ask her a few questions of their own. The man wanted a Giant Schnauzer; the girlfriend a smaller one.

'Look! He's not all *that* big!' he said to the young woman as they waited. The girlfriend smiled but she wasn't convinced. She was wearing black tights, knee-high boots, and a black dress printed with little Scottie dogs. After Caroline had answered the young man's questions about Giant Schnauzers, the girlfriend nodded at her and tried to move him along. As they walked off, her boyfriend was still insisting, 'He's not *that* big.'

Lynne, another Lort Smith volunteer, arrived back at the stand after a walk through the stalls with her dog. Galahad, a tall, elegant Irish Wolfhound with a flowing coat and regal look about him, made Ralf appear almost small. Irish Wolfhounds are the tallest breed of dog in the world. Lynne, too, is always answering questions about Galahad's stature and breed although no one ever need ask her dog's name—it sparkles in diamanté bling on his collar. Galahad made his way to the back of the stand and sunk down on his haunches—it can be tiring working in crowds and he was retiring by nature, said Lynne.

Ralf's back leg started to shake again—he'd seen a Samoyed in the aisle and wanted to say hello. Its owner gave the Samoyed a sharp tug on the lead to keep it walking. That's the thing about all the dogs at the show, Caroline said, they were all working and you could guarantee that they'd all be well behaved. Several small dogs went past held close to the chests of their owners, some of them wrapped in small, fluffy blankets. One tiny Poodle was wearing what looked like a knitted aviator's helmet.

A petite woman with a face painted to look like a Husky or perhaps a wolf took a huge liking to Ralf, talking to him in her girlish voice, enthralled. 'We can sit together,' she said, as she moved closer to Ralf, placing her hand over Ralf's paw to compare size. She took off her glasses, put them in her tote bag on top of a jumper with dog motifs on it, and took a selfie with Ralf. Caroline offered to take it for her, but no, she was quite happy crouching on the floor with Ralf. The woman eventually moved off, by which time Caroline had learned that she gets up at four in the morning every day to walk her own dogs. A balding man stepped up, admiring Ralf's luxuriant whiskers as he slid a few coins in the container. 'Can I have half his beard?' he joked.

Later on, a man with a Bark Busters logo on his shirt paused as he passed, exchanging a few words with Caroline to the effect that Ralf must have a loud bark. Yes, Ralf once had a barking problem, she said, but all he needed was someone around in the house all day! The man said nothing to this and walked on.

Ralf, by now reclining on one of the doggie beds at the stall across the aisle, looked alert as a pair of Rottweilers came into view, and got up to meet them. The three dogs sniffed each other's noses and rear bits as Caroline and their owners compared notes about their respective pets, what they feed them and their weight—the Rotties weighed about 53 kilograms each. As they chatted, the stallholders around them started to pack up. Suddenly there was the loud clack of something hitting the wooden floor. The Rottweilers jumped with fright and spun around on all fours; Ralf didn't flinch. 'That's his training,' explained Caroline.

The crowd passing the stands was thinning, streaming out to the gardens and heading for home to their own pets or to discuss potential pet purchases. Caroline handed over her fundraising tin for the day and made her way with Ralf towards where Sam was waiting to pick them up, knowing as she did that there would be a few more dollars going towards Lort Smith's work and that a few more people would be aware of its work.

The Dog Lovers Show was just one of Ralf's official duties—he was often called on by Lort Smith to help out at its fundraising days. Donations are a vital source of income to the not-for-profit animal welfare centre. Caroline once collected money at an AFL match at Etihad Stadium, Ralf appearing on the banner opening the match, among pictures of other doggie volunteers.

Emma Morgan, Lort Smith's Major Donor and Bequests Manager, recalls spending several hours with Caroline and Ralf on a fundraiser in the Bourke Street Mall in November 2013.

'Ralf was centre of that show,' says Emma. 'People were stopping and talking and donating, not because of Caroline and me in our Lort Smith shirts but because of Ralf. His effect on people is pretty incredible.'

'Everyone wants to work near Ralf,' says CEO Liz Walker.

During that day in the mall, Melbourne's Lord Mayor, Robert Doyle, happened to wander by and, as the other volunteers wondered whether to approach him, Caroline walked over to Lord Mayor, chatted to him and received a donation. At one stage, the Lort Smith group noticed a young girl in a wheel-chair propelling herself determinedly across from the other side of the mall towards them, looking elated. She'd been admiring the Myer Christmas window with her family when she'd recog-nised Ralf; the girl had been a patient at The Royal Children's Hospital. Ralf automatically put his head on her lap.

'But dogs can't talk—so as much as it was Ralf drawing in the crowd, it was Caroline providing the stories,' says Emma. 'I mean, she's telling them that Ralf's married, talking about how he's got kids! People are like, "What?!" Caroline's consistently awesome.'

Caroline had become known by staff at Lort Smith as a highly committed worker, turning up week after week when many others came once a fortnight, a month or less often. She never knocks back an extra request to appear somewhere with Ralf on behalf of the organisation. It takes real dedication and self-motivation to do that, the Lort Smith staff say.

When Emma wanted to take a couple who were major Lort Smith donors to The Royal Children's Hospital to show them the dog therapy work in action, she chose Caroline and Ralf as ambassadors. 'We took the couple on the rounds to show the effect Ralf has on people. People were coming up, very excited to see Caroline and Ralf, saying hi to Ralf,' says Emma, who admits she was rather impressed herself. 'The couple are very reserved but they said later how much they'd enjoyed the visit.'

In August 2013, the Lort Smith recorded a video on pet therapy at The Royal Children's Hospital. Liz Walker accompanied Caroline, Ralf and another volunteer and their dog on the day, the first time she'd seen Ralf at work in the hospital. At one point as they walked along the corridor, a middle-aged woman veered towards them, sank to her knees in front of Ralf, threw her arms around him and started weeping. As Liz was trying to take it all in, Caroline moved quickly to the woman's side, squatted down beside her and said, 'I think you might need a bit of animal therapy.' She offered the woman a tissue—she carries a packet for such times, as well as her 'goo pusher' of disinfectant for her and children's hands. Liz stood back and watched as Caroline comforted the woman, talked to her for some time and then accompanied her to the room where the woman's daughter lay. She soon reappeared and beckoned Liz in. By this stage Ralf was on the bed with the teenage girl, surrounded by both parents, a sister and grandparents. Ralf was obviously enjoying being the centre of the attention and the teenage girl looked pleased. By the tone of the room, it had been a tough day.

Liz saw many other visits and greetings by Ralf and Caroline that day, but that one will always stay with her.

Many dogs like children, she says, but not to the same degree as Ralf—he seemed to get a sense of comfort from them. 'What Ralf does around children is most uncommon,' says Liz. 'And it's clear that Ralf and Caroline have something that's very special.'

In May 2013, Caroline was asked by Megan Nutbean if she'd come to the Lort Smith Annual General Meeting. Ralf was welcome, too, of course. As ever, Caroline replied that, yes, she'd love to attend, even though Lort Smith AGMs weren't part of her usual round of engagements. She assumed that she was 'doing a meet and greet' there or would be asked to talk to an important donor or guest, as sometimes happened at both Lort Smith and The Royal Children's Hospital.

On the afternoon of the AGM, she set off to Southbank for the event, being held in the NAB building, with her freshly washed pet. She parked at what should have been a short walk away but which took about half an hour as CBD workers on their lunch breaks stopped to talk and have their photos taken with Ralf. Caroline also got waylaid in the foyer by people she heard saying, 'There's Ralf!' Liz Walker met Caroline and ushered her into the auditorium, asking her to sit with the Lort Smith staff in the front row.

'Are there any small children near where we'll be sitting?' Caroline asked, worried that Ralf would get bored and restless. 'He'll be okay if you can find a child for him to sit with.'

Liz thought hard and remembered that a woman with a toddler would be sitting in that row.

As the audience took its seats and Caroline sat down with Ralf, she noticed that the child was a fair distance away. Ralf, who'd been told he was working, started scanning the room for small people, his leg quivering as he saw the little boy. As the meeting began he set off down the row. Caroline, knowing it was useless to try to hang onto him, passed the lead to the next person, who passed it to the person next to them, and so on along the row. Having visited the boy,

Ralf turned his attention to the other end of the row. Then he sighted another dog in the middle row. Caroline, by now holding his lead again, tried to hang on as Ralf moved off, but gave up and the lead was passed along until Ralf reached Peter Hitchener, the respected Melbourne newsreader and Lort Smith ambassador, where Ralf stopped. Peter was quite happy to have Ralf sit with him but Ralf was keen to meet the other dog so hauled Peter to his feet; Peter hung on. Ralf kept pulling, succeeding in dragging Peter along until they reached Liz Walker, who whispered, 'Would you like me to take him?'

'Yes, I think that would be nice,' he whispered back.

'Here,' Liz said to Caroline, handing her Ralf's lead, 'you can have this!'

Near the end of the meeting, the vice-president of the board, Samantha Baillieu, addressed the audience to announce the Lort Smith Volunteers of the Year award. Two winners were chosen each year from the 500 volunteers on the recommendations of the volunteer coordinators.

Caroline was shocked as she heard Samantha read out her name and then talk of the significant contribution she and Ralf had made to the program, outlining some of the effects of their work at The Royal Children's Hospital. 'Ralf is known to have a special impact on the children he visits. We are very grateful for Caroline's commitment and dedication to helping Lort Smith and are pleased to present her with an award for 2013 Volunteer of the Year.'

An overawed Caroline was asked to the stage to accept her award. *Please don't make me speak!* she thought. *Please make me invisible!* Samantha, smiling broadly, presented Caroline with a certificate honouring her and an engraved pen. Ralf was given a new Lort Smith bandana.

As the audience dissolved and milled around the foyer chatting after the event, Liz took Ralf to mingle with the crowd so that Caroline could talk to the people wanting to meet her. Caroline was touched by the honour. 'You really only want to be thanked occasionally for what you do, but the Lort Smith makes you feel really supported,' she says. 'Everyone's got your back and that's lovely.'

Volunteering is a joy for her. 'You walk in and you're going to make the family's day a bit easier—it's a pleasure that not everyone gets to have. And every minute you put in, you get back ten minutes of reward, if not more.'

Lort Smith hosts a lunch twice a year to thank their 'vollies', a chance for them all to get together, sometimes to meet other volunteers for the first time. One such event was held in the football clubrooms at the Edinburgh Gardens in North Fitzroy, inner-city Melbourne. It was a glorious late autumn day. Russet and gold leaves formed swathes under the European trees spread throughout the gardens, some ponderous grey-bottomed clouds banked in the distance but stayed there. The volunteers and their pets who made their way across the lawns towards the old-style clubrooms where the event was held looked unremarkable—there were dogs everywhere in the park, dozens of them. Edinburgh Gardens has an off-leash area and is known as being dog-friendly. A group of French Bulldog enthusiasts milled around nearby, at the end of every lead was a seemingly identical black and white dog.

The Lort Smith canines, by contrast, were a jumble of breeds and personalities.

A pair of Jack Russells was among the first to arrive, throwing themselves at the feet of the early-arriving owners, wriggling madly on their backs, looking up, hoping for a rub on the stomach. Bonnie the Boxer, a big friendly girl, pulled her owner into the room, straining on her lead to say hello to anyone who was nearby. A stick-obsessed dog brought its own entertainment from the park. As each volunteer arrived at the clubrooms, decked out in blue-and-white streamers and balloons, they were issued with a nametag marked with the owner's name first then the dog's. Platters of hot finger food were arranged on long trestle tables. Wet noses sniffed vigorously. Jars holding doggie lollypops were deposited in the middle of each table. Bonnie stood watching, a long column of slobber dangling from her mouth.

The volunteers chose a seat or stood balancing their plates of food with one hand, holding their leads with the other. Further over on an outside table, a freshly combed little dog with a feathery tail sat contentedly on her owner's lap while the woman ate lunch and conversed with others at the table. A pair of matching Labradors wearing their blue bandanas dropped side by side next to the table with their owners; the dogs' eyes tracking closely every movement of food from hand to mouth.

A blind retriever walked in with her owner, who is her 'seeing eyes'. Boris, the Doberman, with his sculpted torso, gleaming coat and fine curling tail, was off his lead and investigating the area near the kitchen and under the trestle table. Many of the dogs, like Boris, were big enough to raid the tables; none did. Galahad the Irish Wolfhound arrived a little later, looking impossibly lanky and long of body among the variety of other dogs, one of three Irish Wolfhounds that came on the day.

The occasional person could be heard asking other volunteers where Ralf was. 'He's the hero,' explained one woman. 'Everyone talks about Ralf!' Caroline and Ralf were on their way, delayed by a birthday breakfast for one of the kids. Someone else confused another large black dog, Harley the Groodle, for Ralf, but when Ralf walked in, there was no mistaking him. He entered like an elder statesman. Dignified and stout.

Ralf took a passing interest in the other dogs as he looked around for a child. He'd been told he was 'working' that day. Little Luna, a small chocolate-brown Poodle-cross, bounced over to bark at him, but Ralf raised his snout in the air out of reach of her nose, his attention turning to a nearby vegetable samosa.

Caroline was soon joined by Sherrill, whom she had met in a park in Kew one day. Sherrill, who was new to Victoria, was walking her English Setter, Max, at the time. The women got talking. 'Max looks like he's got a good temperament,' said Caroline. 'Why don't you do some voluntary pet therapy work with him?' That was months before. Caroline didn't see Sherrill in the park again and was thrilled to meet her at the lunch. Sherrill and Max had been volunteering at the renal unit of St Vincents Hospital. 'Max tends to lie down, while I chat,' Sherrill says of their visits. 'He's a good way of introducing yourself.' The patients Sherrill saw spend four to five hours having dialysis, some of them three times a week. 'They say it means life for them.' The patients' arms have tubes attached so they're not able to move enough to reach down to pat a dog but they're always up for a chat, she says. 'You find out something new about them every week. Then they go.'

Barry, a long-term volunteer with the Lort Smith, brought with him his matching Blue Roan Cocker Spaniels, Daisy and Darby. The dogs, brother and sister, had been going to the Heidelberg Repatriation Hospital with him for thirteen years from the time they were fourteen months old. They were always so keen to get to the wards that they'd drag Barry all the way from the underground car park to the lift and up through the hospital to the right ward. Barry had temporarily stopped his visits and was acting as a volunteer driver with Lort Smith. He says Daisy and Darby thought they were going to the hospital on the morning of the volunteers' lunch, pressing their noses against the car window, trying to detect any familiar smells that might suggest they were heading there. 'They know when they're going to the hospital—they start whimpering and making little excited noises,' he says.

Barry recalled fondly the times in the hospital that people sharing an elevator with him would audibly whisper, 'He's got a dog!', and when the daughter-in-law of an elderly patient exclaimed one day, 'These dogs have got hair like Mum!' He said one Vietnamese woman who hadn't spoken in three weeks astounded the nurses by taking one look at his dogs before bending over to talk to them in a stream of Vietnamese.

As Barry talked, a flurry of growling and snarling broke out between several dogs at one end of the clubroom. Even therapy dogs have their differences, it seems. Barry, who was an instructor at an obedience club, said that he and the others running that club were always on the lookout for dogs that were getting too close to each other as their owners conversed—dogs eyeballing each other was often a sign that a fight was about to erupt.

After a period of socialising and chatting, Liz Walker addressed the gathering, speaking of Lort Smith's new 'branding'. Amid the jangle of leashes, panting and the occasional yap, she explained that the organisation covered so much more than its title as 'Animal Hospital'. Its logo would now say 'Lort Smith, Caring for Animals' to reflect the breadth of its work; as she spoke, an image of the logo beamed on a large screen. The mission: To improve the health and happiness of animals and the people who care for them. At this juncture Boris wandered across the screen to sniff Liz, to much laughter. A new image appeared on the screen—Caroline and Ralf, representing pet therapy.

Official business aside, a raffle was drawn and a group photo taken on a knoll outside, a busy, happy if somewhat haphazard shot. The group dispersed as owners and pets wandered back out through the park. Caroline let Ralf off his lead and he trotted away, another engagement over, back in 'dog mode'. She says he was somewhat underwhelmed by the function because he was expecting to see children there.

26

RALF, THE PERFECT PATIENT

Life in the Lovick family was humming along in early January 2014, when Caroline noticed that there was something wrong with Ralf's hind leg.

Alice was at university doing a double arts degree; Imogen was working in reception at a doctor's surgery; Rebecca had finished school and was soon going to the University of Minnesota, US, on a rowing scholarship for four years; Ed was about to start Year 12 and was competing at an elite level of kayaking; Sam had just finished a law degree; and Caroline was running the whole busy household and devoting time to The Royal Children's Hospital and Lort Smith. She was approaching her fiftieth birthday.

'I can't believe I'm turning fifty soon,' she says one day, as if suddenly startled by the fact, doing a few teen-type dance moves with her arms to prove her youthfulness. She and Ralf were in their seventh year as therapy dog and handler.

Fitzy, the cat, had died of kidney failure and another cat joined the family.

Esky had been abandoned in a drink cooler near Imogen's work. She was no beauty—her joints and muscles looked out of whack, her legs were bowed, her hips at the wrong angle, she was covered in old scars, with marks around her neck that suggested she'd been wrapped in wire or thin rope. Esky clearly didn't like people. But she liked Imogen. She would sit quietly as Imogen stroked and talked to her. Anyone else copped a round of hissing, screeching and swiping claws. Caroline says her daughter Imogen, like Sam, is something of a cat whisperer.

Imogen took the bedraggled animal to the local council to see if they had heard from her owner and was asked to leave her details with them. A few days later there was a call from the council. 'We can't even get a hand on this cat, would you come in and get her? She's going to be put down if you don't take her.'

So Imogen drove back to the council pound, picked up Esky, and took her back to the flat she was sharing with her boyfriend at the time. When she returned to live with the family later, Esky came, too.

Taking in unwanted animals was a tradition in both Caroline's and Sam's families. It's like volunteering, Caroline says, you grow up believing that it's a worthwhile thing to do. One-eyed Prudence, of Caroline's childhood, had been a rescue cat. Esky had had a tough life; the family felt that the least they could do was care for her in her latter years. Caroline fed her little pouches of cat food, administered throughout the day in small portions because Esky's ageing teeth were misshapen and she couldn't manage hard feed, waiving her own rule about buying anything other than dry feed for the pets. (Treats and leftovers, of course, don't count.) She would arrange a blanket in a sunny spot by the window for her.

The cranky cat gradually became used to the other members of the family—all nine of them—although that didn't mean she got on with them. She ruled Ralf and Ivy, hissing roundly at them when they encroached on her space and taunting them by sitting in front of the dog door first thing in the morning, refusing to let them out when they wanted to relieve themselves. 'Ralf was almost crossing his legs he wanted to get outside so much! He whines when she does it—and Ralf never whines!' says Caroline. Eventually Esky would allow a dog to sit on the end of her blanket—as long as they don't get too close. They were, after all, her allies at times—when the neighbour's cats started to terrorise her, coming into the Lovicks' property to look for her, Ralf and Ivy chased them out again. Esky stood by and watched. *See, I've got dogs!*

She and the small grey tabby, Kitty, never got on and still live at opposite ends of the house to each other, brawling occasionally when they meet in the middle, which upsets the dogs who join in barking. Kitty gets on better with the canines, sometimes coming up to smooch Ralf—then swiping him with her paw for good measure afterwards.

Esky's behaviour around strangers barely improved. When Imogen dropped her off at Lort Smith not so long ago for a check-up, a vet was soon on the phone to her. 'She won't even let us touch her. Would you mind coming in while we give her the physical?'

In early 2014, Ralf was ten, elderly in Giant Schnauzer years. The fur on his back and flanks was flecked with grey. He had assumed a professorial look about him. His movements were more sedate than they once were and he was no longer nimble enough to catch birds in the backyard, although he'd still try to chase them when they were overhead. He sometimes eased himself into the pool by stepping down onto its ledge before paddling out, with all the caution of a human bather who goes in up to the knees first, while Ivy took running jumps into the water. Sometimes he'd just stand at the water's edge and play with leaves as they passed, pawing the water to bring them closer, while Ivy swam around after the floating metal ball.

Ralf had become even more relaxed about obeying commands. His enthusiasm for food, though, was unabated.

He started the day with a cooked meal (or part of it), joining the family for breakfast and sitting next to Ed, looking adoringly up at him as he ate his bacon and eggs, waiting for a leftover scrap of bacon. (He'd already been fed the rind by Caroline.) 'Ralf couldn't sit any closer to Ed than if he was sitting on his lap!' she says. Very occasionally, Ralf's instinct for food gets the better of him and he slips up. He came bounding up to greet Caroline at the front door one day, when she'd been out, with the rubbish bin lid still lodged on his head.

But Caroline had noticed at The Royal Children's Hospital that Ralf was starting to have trouble with his back leg. She was helping him up onto a bed next to a patient one day when he made a little squeak, as if in pain. She suspected arthritis.

Arthritis isn't unusual in old dogs but as a working dog Ralf needed to be fully mobile, to be able to stand on his rear legs at the edge of the bed, and to be able to climb smoothly up onto it to see a child who might not be able to reach him. Every movement controlled. Caroline didn't want him to ever be in pain, either, so decided to act immediately.

She took Ralf to Lort Smith on 5 January to have him checked. She was sure that if it were arthritis, something could be done for it and Ralf would continue working in the wards. He'd always been a healthy dog, never going to the vet, after being desexed, for anything other than a check-up and his annual shots. So she drove him to Lort Smith with her usual happy anticipation at seeing Liz, Megan and the others there.

Dr Patrick Cheah, Head Vet of Outpatients, greeted Caroline and Ralf in the foyer with his characteristically genial smile, and showed them into a consulting room, a typically utilitarian affair with a stainless-steel examination table in the centre.

Ralf, who was the first Giant Schnauzer Patrick had ever seen—'Bigger than some of the people who work here!'—had always been well mannered in his surgery and happy to see him. Patrick, who'd worked at Lort Smith for twenty years, had seen all kinds of other behaviour—anxious dogs piddling on the table or trying to jump off it mid-examination, dogs snapping in fear, growling or, at worst, lunging at him. There are other animals, though, that are more likely to cause injury—cats are faster, lashing out at you with their claws; and ferrets have nasty, sharp little fangs, he says, and also a 'distinctive and unique' odour, as Patrick charitably calls it.

Ralf, the perfect patient

Patrick had been interested from a veterinary point of view to find out that the tremor in Ralf's back legs was just contained excitement—something he'd wondered about when he first noticed it. He knew that Ralf was on the Lort Smith therapy dog team and previously had heard about his work with children through Caroline and others at Lort Smith. Patrick had attended the AGM the year before, sitting near Caroline and Ralf, and had watched in amusement as Ralf made his way along the first row of the auditorium to greet everyone sitting in it.

He listened to Caroline's description of the discomfort Ralf had shown, felt his legs and confirmed what she thought. He suggested two options to treat the arthritis: anti-inflammatory tablets or a course of Pentosan injections, an expensive anti-arthritic drug that helps lubricate the joints and slow the rate of cartilage degeneration. Caroline chose the latter, feeling like she was 'cracking a walnut with a sledge hammer' over what were such slight symptoms, but wanting to make sure that if Ralf had arthritis he avoided any pain. Patrick reassured her that Ralf would do well on the treatment. He would administer the course of injections, one a week over four weeks, and also prescribe anti-inflammatory drugs to make him more comfortable until the Pentosan took effect. He gave Ralf his first shot and bid dog and owner farewell until the next visit.

But when Caroline brought Ralf in for his third treatment, she had something else to report. Ralf had been getting out of the four-wheel-drive and had tripped then started limping on his right foreleg. Caroline couldn't find anything wrong with his paw or leg when she'd looked at it but Ralf was obviously uncomfortable, she told Patrick. Patrick felt the paw, noted that it was sensitive but couldn't see any swelling.

'It looks more or less normal,' he said. 'I think he's stubbed it and the knock has caused a soft tissue injury. He'll need to get some rest and I'll give you some pain relief for it.'

Caroline decided to give Ralf a break from visiting The Royal Children's Hospital—the priority was getting him fit again.

At home Ralf seemed subdued. He was limping markedly. When she took him to the animal hospital on 26 January for his last Pentosan injection, she told another vet—Patrick wasn't in attendance that day—that Ralf was still sore in his front leg. The vet was surprised—it shouldn't have taken that long for a stubbed toe to settle down—and recommended having the leg X-rayed to check that there wasn't something else wrong. The vet upped the pain relief with a supplementary medication and booked Ralf in for an X-ray in the following week.

Ralf hadn't improved by the next day, even with the additional pain relief. Caroline brought him back to the hospital, this time seeing vet David Hookey. It was decided that Ralf would be admitted as a matter of urgency to examine and X-ray the toe while he was under anaesthetic.

Caroline agreed but she was anxious. She had a feeling that something more serious was wrong with Ralf. She reads Ralf well, says Imogen, as he does her. 'What if it's something more than the toenail?' Caroline asked. That Ralf might have cancer was something she and Sam had already discussed.

'Well, then they'd amputate his toe,' David replied.

Caroline looked down at Ralf and back at David, worrying about what would happen if Ralf needed more than a toe removed. She thanked David, touched Ralf lightly on the top of the head, and left him behind at Lort Smith for the night, walking out through its foyer as if she were in a trance. She went over to her car, sat in the front seat, and sobbed.

Patrick was in the surgery the next day and performed the X-ray on Ralf. He found the cause of Ralf's soreness; the nail on his middle toe was detached from the bone and was hanging from the quick by a thread. A small but nonetheless painful injury. It's not unusual for dogs to catch their nail on something, particularly if the nail is long, and for one to break either partially or completely; because Ralf's nail had broken internally, it appeared to be attached. The nail itself was quite hollow, 'dead', Patrick said. But there was no evidence of bone cancer, he added. Given Ralf's history of tripping and knocking his foot, it seemed that the nail was the cause of the problem.

Ralf was given a local anaesthetic and Patrick removed the dead nail relatively easily with a bit of wiggling. Underneath was a large amount of discharge and pus, suggesting the toe was swollen from infection, which was contributing to the pain Ralf experienced. The nail bed was flushed, dressed and bandaged and Ralf was prescribed a course of antibiotics.

On the morning of the operation Caroline texted Megan Nutbean and told her that Ralf had been admitted to Lort Smith. 'Could you give him cuddles from me, please?'

Megan assured her that she would, and went into the hospital with colleagues Sarah and Jessie to find Ralf. 'This huge dog was in a little cage,' says Megan. Ralf seemed calm but a little less sure of himself than he normally was, she observed. The three women visited him again at lunchtime, and in every break they had, patting his muzzle through the cage door. Caroline called three or four times during the day to see how he was, urged on by her worried children.

She picked up Ralf on 29 January, relieved and happy to be reunited with him, and was given antibiotics to administer and told that the toe should heal within the week. Ralf could be spared the indignity of having to wear an 'Elizabethan collar'—the awkward cone-shaped plastic shield worn round a pet's collar to stop it biting, licking or scratching a wound—if the Lovicks kept an eye on him. Caroline booked him in for a post-operative check-up and to have the bandage removed on 5 February.

The Lovick family began a roster to watch Ralf, all of them on three-hourly shifts to make sure he rested, was supervised if he went outside and that he didn't gnaw at the bandage. Ralf was allowed to sleep on the bed of whoever was on the night shift, who would then have to take him outside if he needed to relieve himself, then make sure he didn't creep into either Ed or Rebecca's beds where he usually slept (their beds were bigger).

Ralf wasn't his usual self the following week: out of sorts, clumping around the house with his sore paw looking like a clubfoot. He seemed unsure of himself and sluggish. Caroline watched for progress but there didn't seem to be any.

On 5 February she took him back to Lort Smith to have his bandage removed. But when one of the vets cut the rubbery bandage off, they found that the wound had opened and Ralf's toe was still swollen—more than it should have been. The tissue had opened but it looked fairly normal— these things sometimes get worse before they get better, the vet reassured Caroline, prescribing another course of anti-biotics and instructing her to bathe the wound in saltwater.

'We'll leave the bandage off so the wound can air,' the vet said. 'Keep him calm and rested, and he shouldn't be working. Come back in five days and we'll check his foot again.'

So Caroline took Ralf home again. But even allowing for the fact that he'd just had an operation, Ralf still didn't seem right to Caroline in the time after he got back home. The children agreed with her.

On the day he was due to return to Lort Smith for his 'post op' check-up, Ralf tripped again, this time in the hallway, knocking off the newly exposed scab. Caroline and Rebecca watched, alarmed, as blood spurted from the wound then gushed like it was from an opened artery. Blood everywhere. She hurriedly wrapped Ralf's paw in a face-washer and duct-taped it, heaved him into the four-wheel-drive with Rebecca, and drove like a shot into the Lort Smith, blood oozing out of the hastily made bandage.

Vet Nicole McLaughlin quickly ushered them all in and examined Ralf's paw; she wasn't happy with what she saw or heard. By now the toe had ballooned and looked decidedly abnormal. She treated the wound and told Caroline she was concerned that Ralf hadn't recovered as expected after such an operation and that he wasn't responding to antibiotics.

'It could be something else. I'd like to take a sample of tissue from the paw and send it off to the lab for analysis,' she said.

Caroline felt her heart racing.

Nicole used a fine needle to aspirate the lesion, and take a sample, telling Caroline the results would be back the next

day. But it would be best to leave Ralf in the hospital overnight until then, in case he needed further treatment. She told
Caroline that Patrick would see Ralf tomorrow to re-examine
him and talk with Caroline about the results.

Caroline handed over Ralf's lead and went out to the car for
the trip home with Rebecca, feeling numb.

Dinner that night at the Lovicks was uncharacteristically
quiet.

Patrick Cheah saw the email from the lab as he sat down to his
computer the next morning. He'd already checked his diary
and noticed the name Lovick booked in at noon. Patrick had
become uneasy about Ralf, too; he read from the computer
entries that the toe didn't appear to have healed at all in the
ten days since he'd operated on it for a seemingly innocuous
broken nail. The cytology report confirmed his doubts: it
mentioned inflammation, which was to be expected, but also
the presence of 'atypical squamous cells'. This set off more
alarm bells: 'atypical' meant the cells sampled were abnormal
and that usually meant one thing—the toe was most likely
cancerous.

He phoned the Lovicks.

Sam answered the phone and listened as Patrick told him
about the cytology report.

'Given the highly suspicious nature of the tissue from the
report, the best thing to do would be to amputate Ralf's toe,'
he recommended. 'It will become harder to remove if it gets
into his foot. I'm fairly happy that he will respond well but you

have to be careful with a big dog removing a toe because they need to bear more weight on their feet.'

After some discussion, Sam gave permission to proceed with the operation.

Ralf went into surgery straight after that phone call. It was a relatively long procedure, taking about an hour, and not the easiest to perform, says Patrick. 'There are a lot of blood vessels in that part of the paw and they tend to bleed a lot.' He took the whole toe off back to the foot—the swollen tissue was restricted to the front of the toe but it was important to take it back to *clean* tissue so that there wasn't any suspicious tissue left behind. The operation was a success, but it was the biopsy results that would tell them if all the cancer had been removed and determine Ralf's fate.

Ralf was wheeled, groggy, to a cage in Ward Three for the night. Ward Three, where animals recover from surgery, is a dismal place, reeking of strange disinfectant odours and urine. Sitting on a cold tiled floor are eight heavy metal cages, each with some bedding, housing dogs with recently sewn gashes, looking spaced out and fretful. Whenever the door opens it lets in a cacophony of howls, whimpers, wailing, barking and the yowling of cats from down the corridor.

Caroline went in that evening to visit Ralf, taking with her several blankets including a soft, fleecy one that everyone in the family had rubbed on themselves so that Ralf could be surrounded by familiar smells. 'You understand you probably won't get the blankets back,' an assistant said.

'We don't care,' replied Caroline.

When Caroline phoned the hospital the following morning, she was told the vet who'd seen Ralf that day had noted he was no longer uncomfortable on his front leg and that the angry lesion was now gone. She was pleased he was recovering but was still anxious—the results of the test performed on the tumour weren't back yet. It would be another week at least before the Lovicks found out if Patrick had removed all the cancer or whether it had spread. If the cancer kept invading, it would move into tissue in Ralf's leg, then into his lymph nodes, then lungs.

It was a fretful wait. Caroline worried privately, trying to keep up the appearance of being on an even keel for the family. 'I was beside myself.' She rang the Lort Smith staff often to ask how Ralf was. 'He's fine, he's great,' they would tell her. 'We're just keeping him in for observation,' they would say.

Megan and the others kept visiting Ralf in their breaks and although she didn't tell Caroline at the time, she admits now that, 'He looked pretty miserable'.

For Caroline the death of Ralf would mean far more than losing a loved pet; her time in the wards helping children and the years of therapy work with him would come to an abrupt end. 'I can't go in as me,' she says, 'it's Ralf and me.'

Caroline knew, on a rational level, that Ralf would one day pass the way of all family pets and realised her time with him was finite, but she still wasn't prepared for it. She steeled herself for the worst outcome.

'I feel completely spoilt and privileged that I go to work with Ralf—I've loved every minute of it. It's a little window, a nugget and it's not going to last forever. I feel incredibly lucky to have Ralf in the world.'

She and Sam had to think, too, about how far they'd go with their pet's treatment. The vet's bills were mounting up, costing thousands. 'We weren't sure where we were going with the information. It was scary. We didn't know if we'd have to say to the kids or to me "That's your dog gone".'

Ralf was discharged on 12 February and due back on 20 February for a check-up and to have his bandages removed. An examination before he left showed that the sutures were holding well and that all looked good.

When Caroline picked him up she was greeted by a 'goodbye committee' of Lort Smith women who'd visited Ralf and had also cared for Caroline during his stay, always asking how *she* was. The veterinary nurses had decorated Ralf's bandages with his name and brightly coloured dog bones and heart shapes. Caroline was touched. She'd become part of the close-knit family at the Lort Smith, says Megan, and Ralf was a big part of it, too. They'd become involved with the staff outside Lort Smith activities, for example visiting Lort Smith worker Christine Stankowski and her baby Olivia at The Royal Children's and at home when Olivia was being treated for hip dysplasia.

Ralf, of course, had been a perfect patient. 'He's such a teddy bear of a dog,' says Patrick. 'Even though the experience was painful, he never played up. He was always happy to see you. There's not an aggressive bone in his body.'

If the family's care of Ralf before he was diagnosed with cancer was attentive, it was doubly so when he came home. They continued their 24-hour roster, keeping Ralf comfortable and occupied. The kids weren't allowed to go out if it was their turn to Ralf-sit; instead of Rebecca going out with her friends, they came over to the Lovicks'. The family often sat on the floor so Ralf could lie on the couch. They administered his favourite chewies. It was during a heatwave, so Rebecca damped down some towels for Ralf to lie on while he waited for Ivy to come in from her swim. Ed and Rebecca spent hours rubbing his stomach, as Ralf lay on his back, his eyes rolling with pleasure.

Caroline handed Sam the phone on the day the results of the biopsy were due back. 'You ring.'

When Sam was put through to Patrick, he was told the biopsy results had come in. The lab's report confirmed that the cancer was a malignant tumour—and noted that it was aggressive.

The report also said that the tumour had been completely removed.

Ralf had been saved by a toenail. Had it not been for Caroline's intuition and the broken nail, coincidentally located at the source of his cancer, the tumour would have spread undiscovered. Now Caroline could think about resuming their voluntary work.

She had told Brenda Kittelty that Ralf had cancer, but only Brenda—to have mentioned it more broadly could have upset or worried some of the children or parents who depended on him coming in, as well as hospital staff. She'd tried to keep it within the family, too, but so many people knew Ralf that she was only barely surprised when she was out shopping and greeted by an 'Oh my god, Caroline, how's Ralf?'

Caroline gave Ralf time to recover and to make sure he was ready for work. He swam and she started taking him on walks around the block, checking that he was walking without a limp and then jogging easily. On Thursday 27 February, she made an appointment at Lort Smith to ask a vet's opinion on whether Ralf was fit enough to resume his rounds the following Monday; the vet said yes.

She rang Brenda on the Monday morning to say he'd recovered but that he still had bald patches over parts of his body where he'd been shaved for the injections to be administered and drips attached. And his missing toe was very visible. Ralf's toes were big, like those on the paws of monsters you'd see in Maurice Sendak books. Brenda said to bring him in, even if he had to work a shorter day.

But there was one more test. Caroline pulled her Lort Smith T-shirt out of the drawer and held it up. 'What do you think, Ralfie? Do you want to work?'

Ralf took one look at the T-shirt, heard the word 'work' and his back leg started shaking.

27

A DAY ON
THE WARDS

It is past ten o'clock on Monday morning and Caroline Lovick is walking into The Royal Children's Hospital with Ralf, patches on his legs still stubbly from being shaved during his treatment for cancer. Ralf is instantly on the lookout for children among the people drifting in and out of the hospital.

Caroline greets the people in the lift, including a couple of teenage girls saying, 'It's okay, he's a therapy dog', in case anyone might be concerned about the animal taking up the space of several people. One of the girls, blue-haired and with a pierced eyebrow, is trying not to look interested but she can't help herself. 'How much does he eat?'

Once on the third floor they pick up pace in the corridors, heading for Rosella ward, Paediatric ICU, the first of ten areas they will visit. Caroline now sometimes 'gowns up' to visit the oncology ward, Kookaburra. Oncology was once off-limits to dogs, and only certain dogs and their owners are allowed in there. She and Ralf also sit with patients as they undergo chemotherapy.

They look like a professional outfit; Caroline brisk and businesslike, wearing black trousers and boots with her royal blue Lort Smith shirt; Ralf in his matching blue bandana, moving beside her with a spring in his trot. He's still wearing the name tag sent by Karla of Donegal.

A mother carrying a tiny baby smiles as she catches sight of Ralf. 'What is he?' she asks, bemused. 'He reminds me of a Clydesdale horse!'

Caroline tells the woman about Giant Schnauzers and the work that she and Ralf do. Ralf hasn't stopped looking at the baby. 'No, Ralfie, it's a baby, you can't see a baby!' she reminds him. 'He's baby crazy,' she says, as she takes off again.

Ralf veers towards a canteen worker wearing gloves, who steps back. 'I know Ralf, but not everyone wants to pat you,' says Caroline, correcting his path.

Brenda Kittelty sees the pair arrive at Family Resource from her glass-fronted office and reaches for the plastic container that stores the volunteers' security passes, covered at one end with sticky notes—requests from patients to see a particular dog among them. Brenda now manages fifty-three Lort Smith therapy dog volunteers—up from the dozen or so when Caroline started—among 200 volunteers across twelve organisations.

There are some real canine characters among them. There's Maggie the three-legged Spoodle and Sami, the blind

Labrador. CEO Liz Walker calls Amity, the Standard Poodle, the 'Lollipop Dog', because her white coat is clipped like a corkscrew with the raised fur dyed in different colours. All sizes are represented, from Poppy, the Chihuahua, whose owner dresses in funny outfits, to Biggles, the Old English Sheepdog, who's one of the stars of the Dulux paint ads, and Rebus the Irish Wolfhound. A miniature pony called Koda made some appearances, too. Koda, who was born the size of a cat and is now 59 centimetres tall and weighs 35 kilograms, is famous for his tiny stature. Brenda hasn't received a complaint yet about the dog program since she took it over, but much positive feedback.

After a brief chat to Caroline and a look at Ralf's foot, Brenda tells her which rooms have requested a visit and the pair set off on their rounds.

First call is Rosella ward, ICU. 'Hello, darling,' calls out Kristy Dea from the reception desk. She means Ralf. 'Oh, sorry, Caroline, I didn't mean to ignore you!' she adds as she looks up from patting him.

This happens a lot, says Caroline, amiably. She's even heard herself being referred to as, 'Oh, you know, the woman who comes in with Ralf.'

Greetings and a catch-up over, the dog therapy duo heads into the ward. 'Hello, big boy,' someone calls out as they pass.

Once in Rosella ward Caroline opens the doors of the first room, checking to see if there is a nurse inside. She never enters an ICU room without a nurse. She sticks her head through the door. Ralf's snout appears a few seconds later. A family is clustered around a boy in green pyjamas and dressing gown. The atmosphere is silent and concerned.

'Hi guys, this is Ralf, he's one of the therapy dogs that go around. Would you like a play date with Ralf?'

No one speaks. Then, 'Look, there's a big dog to see you,' says the mother, beckoning them forward.

Caroline and Ralf step politely towards the bed. 'Can this bed go any lower?' she asks, deftly adjusting the bed down until Ralf's head is at the same level. Ralf looks at the pale boy, who's staring into the middle distance. The boy shifts his gaze towards Ralf, who puts his head on the bed, whiskers spreading out on the sheets, eyebrows twitching. The boy draws his arm out slowly from under the sheets, extends his hand and touches the top of Ralf's head with one finger. His parents look at each other and smile quietly.

Caroline pushes the door of the next room ajar. Inside, a slight girl of about ten lies motionless; her face, barely visible behind an oxygen mask, is starkly pale against a mass of long dark hair fanning out on the pillow. Three jagged lines pulsate along an overhead monitor measuring her vital signs. Stands with drip lines containing clear fluids are positioned next to her. Trolleys for used towels and an infectious waste bin stand against the wall. A fan is trained on her bed. A nurse in bright green scrubs and a middle-aged male doctor are discussing levels of oxygen; Caroline catches their eyes and they nod imperceptibly.

'Hi there, do you want a visit from Ralfie?' Caroline asks the girl.

She smiles and coos, 'He's so cute, like a shaggy horse.'

It looks like they're in the middle of a check-up so Caroline mentally notes the room and tells the girl they will return later.

A look of steely concentration crosses her face as she leaves and prepares for the next visit.

Two rooms along a father is tending to his son, who lies listlessly on his back.

'Hello, beautiful, would you like a play date with Ralf?' she asks the boy.

No response from the boy, but the man smiles and rolls his son over onto his side so he's facing Ralf and Caroline. She suggests he lower the bed, too, then the boy catches sight of Ralf. Now there's a glimmer in his eyes. Ralf edges close and rests his head on the bed next to the boy's face. The father moves the boy's arm, thin as a stick, and rubs it against Ralf's neck. The boy's face lights up at the feel of the warm, furry animal. He runs his fingers through Ralf's whiskers.

'He's beautiful, isn't he, Dad?'

Hospital staff, having heard of Ralf's brush with cancer, come up every now and then, pleased to see him again after his absence, fussing over him and asking Caroline about his health.

While they're in ICU, Caroline and Ralf encounter two children who've just had amputations; a girl who's lost part of a leg, and a boy who's missing several fingers.

'Ralfie's had cancer and he's had an amputation, too!' she tells each child, pointing to Ralf's foot.

The children seem delighted, in the accepting way that children are, that Ralf is part of their special club.

Ralf picks up pace as he trots towards Koala ward, the cardiovascular area. A small girl in a red smock, standing at the doorway of a room, sees the dark figure bobbing along with Caroline coming towards her, steps forward for a closer look and then retreats inside as they near. Ralf, sensing her hesitancy, drops to the floor with his head on the ground. 'He's making himself as small as he can be,' explains Caroline, 'so he won't scare you.' But to a three-year-old he's still big and dark. She peeks out, giggles and ventures a little closer. The doctor inside the room is talking with the girl's mother, but after noticing Caroline, he says to the mother, 'Sorry, excuse me for a minute but I just have to pat Ralf!' He leaves the room for a minute or two to say hello before resuming the consultation.

In their next room a girl lies looking up at the ceiling, her head tilted back, held in traction by a 'halo', a metal brace that has been decorated with butterfly stickers, her mouth open. Her father stands by her bed, a down-to-earth chap with an outdoors look about him.

'G'day Ralf, how are you going?' he says, smiling genially, after Caroline introduces them both. The man visibly relaxes, as if his soul has just sighed. His daughter stares on at the ceiling, unable to move her head in her metal scaffolding.

Caroline shifts two plastic chairs to face each other, lifting Ralf's front half onto one, then his back half onto the other. Ralf leans over and puts his head near the girl's shoulder as her father rearranges her arm. As she feels his fur brushing against her skin she laughs softly. Then laughs again. It is like music.

A prepubescent pony-tailed girl sits alone in the neighbouring room. Most children have a parent with them but the older ones are sometimes on their own. She looks pleased to have company and Caroline launches into a lively conversation with her. Has she just come in? Yes, the girl replies. Does she

249

have a dog? No, her father's house is too small, she explains; she just has three brothers. Maybe she could trade one of her brothers for a dog? The girl nods and laughs gleefully.

'This is Ralf and he's here to make you smile.'

'It's working!' says the girl.

Caroline asks the girl if she has a mobile phone with her so she can take a photo of her with Ralfie on it. The girl replies that she doesn't have her phone and Caroline says, 'Well, you'll just have to remember him.'

'I'll remember!' the girl says.

Caroline and Ralf move on to reception at Cockatoo ward, which specialises in surgical and neurological care. Old friend Susie Knight sees them coming and grins.

'Mate, you've not been well?' she says to Ralf. Susie has become the owner of a young Rottweiler and proceeds to tell Caroline about its puppy training, asking her for advice on some of the finer points. 'How do I get my dog to be like Ralf!'

Caroline offers to help her with the training and quickly asks if there's anywhere Ralf can't go today before Susie answers an incoming call.

The children in Cockatoo ward are usually older, sometimes teenagers. A long-haired girl of perhaps twelve looks up from her computer game and greets Caroline. The open shelves on the wall opposite her are covered in a party of soft toys, bright metallic balloons fan out on strings from the floor.

'Can Ralf schmooze on your bed?' Caroline asks.

'Sure,' she replies, as Ralf climbs up over the steel bars and settles in next to her.

A day on the wards

'He's cute but he's big!' the girl says.

'Yes, we had to get a bigger bed for my son because Ralf takes up so much room,' says Caroline.

The girl looks surprised. The idea of buying a bed to accommodate a dog is clearly a new concept. Caroline talks to her about her schoolwork and how she does it in hospital, offering some tips. Ralf eyes the round plastic container of food on the tray next to her—but only for an instant.

Outside, in the corridor, an amiable bearded man in long robes and with a Turkish accent strikes up a conversation with Caroline as he waits for his wife and two young daughters to come out of the room behind him.

'They've never seen a dog before,' he says of his daughters.

'Here, want to take him?' he jokes, pointing at Ralf. The girls smile shyly.

'Is he on Valium?' the man asks. 'He's so quiet.'

He squats down to look Ralf in the face, obviously taken by him.

'How much does he eat?'

Next door, an older teen sits by herself in a darkened room. She tells Caroline it's her last day on antibiotics. 'Wow, that's wonderful!' says Caroline, without asking why the girl was on antibiotics. It's enough to know that the news is good.

Ralf climbs up on the vinyl day bed with the girl, who's sitting in the corner, her knees folded. Soon Caroline and the girl are talking about schoolwork; the girl is concerned about falling behind, and Caroline tells her that she can ask the hospital to get a teacher in to help her. 'It's better than going to a private school!' Caroline says. It's a small tip but perhaps one that could help the girl keep up with her work.

She walks past a couple of rooms, not wanting to interrupt. A woman in the first one is cradling her son, silently, on the divan. In the second room, a family of four sits around a teenage girl who has her back to the door. She is awake but is unwilling or is too sick to talk right now. 'We'll come back,' mouths Caroline.

They move along to see a dark-haired boy of seven, all energy and furious movement. A young snappily dressed female doctor is asking the boy's parents questions as she tries to slip a stethoscope under his pyjama top. The boy jerks his body up and starts rocking. The doctor keeps trying. The boy waves his floppy teddy bear through the air in a few frantic motions, its arms and legs flailing, and hits himself in the head with his other hand.

Caroline introduces Ralf and helps him up onto the bed. The boy is still thrashing around but he's interested. He starts smacking Ralf on the top of his head then pulls down hard on his beard. Ralf doesn't react. Caroline lays Ralf down along the bed as close to the wriggling child as possible as the doctor tries to settle the boy back down on the pillow to try the stethoscope again. Ralf snuggles up close, as Caroline takes the boy's bare foot and rubs it against his fur, stroking Ralf's back as she does. The boy stops smacking and is almost still. The doctor is able to go about her business, tapping the boy's other foot to test his reflexes, taking advantage of his momentary quietness.

'Is he nervous?' the father asks, pointing to Ralf's shaking hind leg.

'No, that's adrenalin,' Caroline tells him. 'It means, "I'm so damn excited and happy, I can't tell you".'

At intervals, Ralf raises his head and looks at Caroline, as if checking in.

The doctor produces a tape measure. 'Shall I do Ralf first?' she says.

'Is he going to grow more?' the boy asks.

Caroline is talking at the same time to the boy's parents, who are looking surprised. 'I can't believe how good he is,' says the father, as entranced by Ralf as his son.

She tells them about a program called Dogs for Kids with Disabilities, which provides specially trained assistance dogs to families. Then she turns back to the boy: 'You're so good!' she tells him. (It's hard when you're young and frustrated all the time, she says later. When so much of what you do doesn't get praised.) The boy sits up as Caroline rolls Ralf onto his back so he can look up at him. 'You can tell he's having a nice time, can't you?' she says to the lad as he pats Ralf.

Caroline eventually prises Ralf off the bed as the boy blows him a kiss then quickly loses interest.

'Thank you, Ralf, you've been such a help,' the doctor says, giving Caroline a knowing look.

Caroline leads Ralf out, leaving the doctor talking to the parents about services available for their son in the community. 'I love those moments when everyone's happy,' she says.

They stop by the Summit Activity Room, where a boy who couldn't be more than six is wheeling around a stand with his drip bag. It's amazing how quickly children learn to do this, Caroline says. Then the pair quicken their pace again to move onto another ward and more rooms.

Their last call is to a dark-haired boy of twelve, who sits fully clothed on his bed, shoes on, iPad on his lap. He looks like

253

he's about to be discharged, Caroline thinks. Then she notices the drip. 'We've got a Retriever,' the mother tells her, 'let's take a photo of Ralf to make him jealous!' The boy strokes Ralf for a while before Caroline squirts some disinfectant on her hands, takes the boys hands in hers and rubs them vigorously.

'You might see us again,' says the mother, 'we'll be here for a few months.'

'Well, they only keep the really gorgeous ones here!' says Caroline. 'We'll be back!'

Caroline leaves sometime after three o'clock—or tries to. Ralf dawdles as they head away from the wards, pulling on his leash in the direction of outpatients as Caroline steers him towards the exit. She gets him through to the atrium but he plants all four paws and won't shift. Caroline hauls on the lead and tries to drag him towards the exit. Ralf lies down and refuses to move. 'It makes me look like a dog abuser trying to drag him around,' she says, laughing.

Ralf is back doing what he loves and doesn't want to stop. Not just yet.

Acknowledgments

Firstly, thanks to Caroline Lovick, without whom the book would not have been possible, for her time and patience. I spent many an enjoyable morning laughing with her over accounts of Ralf's life. Also to Sam Lovick for his witty observations, and the rest of the family for their input. Caroline and Sam generously shared their story with the wish that any royalties from the book go to The Royal Children's Hospital and Lort Smith.

Thanks to those at The Royal Children's Hospital who allowed me to follow Caroline on her visits: Vanessa Whatmough organisationally, and to Brenda Kittelty, Susie Woods and Johnny Millar. The cheery staff at Lort Smith were also wonderful: Megan Nutbean, Liz Walker and Patrick Cheah, among them. Jessie Bainbridge at Trinity Manor was a joy to deal with, too.

Then there were those who shared stories of their part in Ralf's life: Lynda Tyzack, Jenny Moore, Wesley Laird and Harriet Drummond. The parents of the children Ralf visited were instrumental too: Jazmin Hall, Corey Harrison, Chris Wilson and Samantha Brew, prime among them.

In writing this book I found two texts particularly helpful; *In the Company of Animals: A Study of Human-Animal Relationships* by James Serpell (Cambridge University Press, 1996) and Felicity Jack's *The Kindness of Strangers: A History of the Lort Smith Animal Hospital* (Spinifex Press, 2003).

As ever, those at Allen & Unwin were marvellous: thanks to Claire Kingston for her vision, Laura Mitchell for her ever-friendly and sage guidance, and Susin Chow for her insightful editing.

A special mention should be made to the countless volunteers out there who, like Caroline Lovick, make others lives better and the world a happier place.

Acknowledgments from Caroline Lovick

Every volunteer's story is worth retelling, so I would like to thank Anne Crawford and Allen & Unwin for putting Ralf's and mine into words. I would also like to thank all the staff at The Royal Children's Hospital and Trinity Manor for allowing Ralf to pace their wards, and Lort Smith for their unstinting support and the exemplary care they have given to Ralf. In the end, I believe it is what Ralf means to the children that matters; I have seen no better tribute to Ralf than this poem which 11-year-old Amber Lee Jepsen, a patient at the Children's, was moved to write:

> Ralf is a dog who we love and adore
> When he's happy he will shake his paw
> And with a wag of his little stumpy tail
> He'll bring us joy without fail
> Upon our beds he likes to sleep
> Looking like a woolly black sheep
> Demanding hugs is what he does best
> Even while he is having a rest

RALF

But who can resist giving Ralf a hug
On a bed as snug as a bug
And there on our beds he will stay
Until he is dragged quite firmly away
So this is the life of Ralf the Dog
At the wards of the Children's he loves to hog
To us children inside he brings such joy
So much more than our favourite toy
So let us thank Ralf for all of his fun
Because, after all, he's number one.

KYLIE MILLER

Anne Crawford has written or co-written six books, most recently *Women of Spirit* (Allen & Unwin, 2014), *Great Australian Horse Stories* (Allen & Unwin, 2013), *Forged with Flames* (Wild Dingo Press, 2013) and *Doctor Hugh* (Allen & Unwin, 2012).

She was a feature writer for *The Age* and *The Sunday Age* for many years, researched a documentary on South Africa, and is also a published and exhibited photographer. Anne worked in Nepal voluntarily for The Fred Hollows Foundation and is currently a volunteer with the Country Fire Authority. She lives in South Gippsland and owns a Red Heeler-cross called Indi.